THE PYRA

THE PENTAGON

THE GOVERNMENT'S TOP SECRET PURSUIT OF MYSTICAL RELICS, ANCIENT ASTRONAUTS, AND LOST CIVILIZATIONS

THE PYRAMIDS
AND
THE PENTAGON

The Government's
Top Secret Pursuit of
Mystical Relics,
Ancient Astronauts, and
Lost Civilizations

BY
NICK REDFERN

New Page Books
A Division of The Career Press, Inc.
Pompton Plains, NJ

THE PYRAMIDS AND THE PENTAGON
EDITED AND TYPESET BY NICOLE DEFELICE
Cover design by Ian Shimkoviak/the BookDesigners
Printed in the U.S.A.

To order this title, please call toll-free 1-800-CAREER-1 (NJ and Canada: 201-848-0310) to order using VISA or MasterCard, or for further information on books from Career Press.

The Career Press, Inc.
220 West Parkway, Unit 12
Pompton Plains, NJ 07444
www.careerpress.com
www.newpagebooks.com

Library of Congress Cataloging-in-Publication Data
Redfern, Nicholas, 1964-
        The pyramids and the Pentagon : the government's top secret pursuit of mystical relics, ancient astronauts, and lost civilizations / by Nick Redfern.
        p. cm.
        Includes bibliographical references.
        ISBN 978-1-60163-206-7 -- ISBN 978-1-60163-611-9 (ebook) 1. Parapsychology--Government policy--United States. 2.
Official secrets--United States 3. Defense information, Classified--United States. 4. Relics. 5. Mysteries, Religious. 6.
Extraterrestrial beings. 7. Antiquities. 8. Civilization, Ancient. 9. Curiosities and wonders. 10. Conspiracies. I. Title.

BF1040.R427 2012
001.94--dc23
                                                                    2012013334

For Rich Reynolds, for being
a good friend and a voice of
sanity.

ACKNOWLEDGEMENTS

I would like to offer my sincere thanks and deep appreciation to everyone at New Page Books and Career Press, particularly Michael Pye, Laurie Kelly-Pye, Kirsten Dalley, Nicole DeFelice, Gina Talucci, Jeff Piasky, and Adam Schwartz; all of the staff at Warwick Associates for their fine promotion and publicity campaigns; and my literary agent, Lisa Hagan, for her always excellent work.

CONTENTS

IN THE
BEGINNING

In the 1981 movie *Raiders of the Lost Ark*, which starred Harrison Ford as archaeologist Indiana Jones, Nazi hordes were in hot pursuit of the legendary Ark of the Covenant, a mysterious chest said to have housed the Ten Commandments provided to Moses by God on Mount Sinai. Given that the Ark was supposed to possess powers both awesome and devastating, Hitler's intention was to harness those same powers, use them against anyone and everyone who might stand in his way, and take control of the world. Fortunately, things did not go Hitler's way. After a wild adventure that took him from Peru to the United States and from Egypt to an island in the Aegean Sea, Indiana Jones saved the day, wrestled the

Ark out of the clutches of Hitler's minions, got the girl, and all was good. But, it's the final moments of the movie that are the most memorable.

The Pentagon: keeper of ancient mysteries. (Copyright U.S. government.)

After the Nazis were defeated, the Ark of the Covenant was transferred to the United States, where military intelligence personnel assured a pleased and satisfied Jones that the priceless artifact would be studied carefully by the finest minds and scholars available. That assurance, however, was nothing less than a brazen lie. Instead, something very different happened. Unbeknownst to Jones, the Ark was *not* studied. The U.S. government, perhaps fearful of unleashing the incredible forces the Ark possessed, took what it considered to be the wisest and safest course of action: The Ark was placed into a wooden crate, which was then carefully and firmly sealed, and

taken to a secure warehouse away from any and all pry-
ing eyes and inquiring minds. The government was intent on keeping the genie firmly in the bottle, so to speak,
never again to be released.

Raiders of the Lost Ark was, and more than 30 years after its release still is, a work of highly entertaining fiction.
The deep and secret involvement of the U.S. government
in the study of ancient artifacts, religious relics, and
numerous archaeological wonders, however, is most assuredly *not* fiction. In the pages that follow, you will learn
of astounding official knowledge of, and secret quests
to seek out the truth behind Noah's Ark, the Dead Sea
Scrolls, the magical history of Stonehenge, tales of nuclear warfare in the distant past, prophecies of the Mayans,
and much more. It is a wild and amazing story that spans
millennia and takes us from the heart of the pyramids to
the depths of the Pentagon.

DEAD SEA
DISCOVERIES

In terms of key and integral world events, 1947 was a year of profoundly deep and significant proportions. United States President Harry S. Truman signed the National Security Act, which paved the way for the creation of the Central Intelligence Agency (CIA). The first, priceless collection of what have famously become known as the Dead Sea Scrolls was found in caves at Qumran, an ancient and historic site on the West Bank. At the White Sands Proving Ground, New Mexico, a collection of fruit flies made history when they became the first living creatures to reach the fringes of space, after being blasted into the skies above aboard a captured German World War II–era V-2 rocket. The age of the flying saucer was famously ushered in, after American pilot Kenneth Arnold witnessed nine strange-looking aircraft flying close to Mount Rainier, Washington State. And, many UFO researchers believe an alien spacecraft crashed on harsh, remote desert land outside Roswell, New Mexico. Singular, unconnected events in a world constantly in a state of change, development, and wonder? Or integral parts of a greater, and very old, puzzle guided by the mysterious hands of destiny, fate, and grand design? Most people would probably say the former. But, sometimes, the majority are wrong—devastatingly so, even.

Secrets of the Caves

Close to 1,000 in number, the Dead Sea Scrolls represent a veritable treasure-trove of early written material from almost every book of the Old Testament, chiefly dating from around 150 BC to 70 BC. Their amazing discovery dates back to February 1947, when, along with his young cousin, Muhammad edh-Dhib, then only a teenager, stumbled across a series of caves at Qumran on the northwest side of the Dead Sea, which borders Jordan to the east, and Israel to the west. Upon exploring one particular cave, edh-Dhib was amazed to find a number of ancient texts, carefully and faithfully recorded on aged parchment. edh-Dhib excitedly scooped up the items and, with his cousin in tow, raced back home to his family's Bedouin camp to show them his discovery. It didn't take long before word got around that something unusual had been unearthed. In fact, matters began to spiral with extraordinary speed when talk of the scrolls began to heat up in and around Bethlehem, particularly when more scrolls were found in 11 other caves, and throughout a period of time that extended up until 1956.

Those immediate times after edh-Dhib's discovery were distinctly wild and turbulent ones. The Syrian Orthodox Church expressed its firm interest in seeing the scrolls, as did representatives of the American Schools of Oriental Research. Interested parties in the Vatican secretly negotiated to buy some of the scrolls; others in the field of biblical archaeology scrambled to see them and examine them; and some scholars called for the scrolls to be placed under official control and oversight, lest they be spread far and wide, possibly even becoming catastrophically lost or destroyed.

Due to circumstances provoked by the turbulent Arab-Israeli War of 1948, the scrolls were hastily transported to Lebanon for safe-keeping. Six years later, they were up for sale and were ultimately sold for $250,000 and transferred to the Rockefeller Museum in Jerusalem. Then, after the Six-Day War of 1967, the scrolls ended up at the Shrine of the Brook, an arm of the Jerusalem-based Israel Museum, where they continue to reside to this very day. There is, however, yet another story of the Dead Sea Scrolls. It is one filled with, and fueled by, dark conspiracy and involves none other than the CIA.

An Encounter at the Embassy

While extraordinary findings were being made at Qumran, historic events were unfolding in the United States. Back in late 1944, William J. Donovan, who was the founder of the Office of Strategic Services (OSS), arguably the earliest incarnation of what eventually became the CIA, mused upon the idea of establishing the ultimate intelligence-gathering agency. It was designed to act as the nation's focal point for securing and analyzing data relevant and vital to U.S. national security and the defense of the nation. The ambitious idea was of great interest to the president, Franklin D. Roosevelt. With the battle still on to defeat Germany, Italy, and Japan, however, survival was the primary name of the game. It was not until July 26, 1947, two years after world peace had been restored, that this ultimate secret agency finally came into being, when Roosevelt's successor, Harry S. Truman, passed the National Security Act. The Central Intelligence Agency was duly born.

The very idea that the newly created CIA might have played an integral, albeit deeply clandestine, role in the saga of the Dead Sea Scrolls sounds manifestly bizarre in the extreme. But, in this particular case, the old adage about truth being far stranger than fiction really does apply. As an example of the speed with which the CIA became a major player on the world stage, within weeks of its establishment, its coiling tentacles had spread far and wide. A sizeable number of its newly recruited staff had previously been employed as deep-cover, overseas operatives and assets in the wartime Office of Strategic Services (OSS) and the Central Intelligence Group (CIG). Many of them, therefore, were already in place to ensure the successful growth of the CIA's new presence and influence at a global level.

One of those who went on to play an intriguing and significant role in the formative years of the CIA—and who had previously served with the Strategic Services Unit (the remnants of the OSS) and the Counter-Intelligence Corps (CIC)—was Miles Axe Copeland, Jr. Back in 1947, Copeland was working to both develop and further expand U.S. interests in the ancient city of Damascus, the capital of Syria. In fact, Copeland was nothing less than the CIA's station officer there—a prestigious position, indeed. Agency personnel are trained to deal with unpredictability, with do-or-die decisions, and with breaking, escalating events. But, perhaps, even Copeland was unprepared for what was certainly the most memorably odd experience of his time spent in old Damascus.

On one particular morning in the fall of 1947, a mysterious Egyptian merchant quietly knocked on the door of Copeland's office, which was housed innocuously in the confines of the American Embassy. Dressed in flowing Bedouin robes, the somewhat-Machiavellian visitor came bearing a gift: It was a very old, and somewhat decayed, rolled-up parchment displaying text in a language that Copeland did not recognize. Copeland watched carefully as the man unrolled the material and listened intently as his purpose for turning up at the Embassy was explained: The man wanted U.S. officialdom's help in deciphering the aged material. Copeland, his interest now piqued, took a close look at it. Maybe it was written in Hebrew or Aramaic; given that he was not fluent in either, Copeland wasn't altogether sure. But he had a friend and colleague who surely would know: Kermit Roosevelt, a director of the Institute of Arab American Affairs, a significant figure in the CIA's Middle Eastern division, and a man who was fluent in both Hebrew and Aramaic. The Egyptian was seemingly satisfied and pleased that Roosevelt would likely be able to help him in his quest to have the texts translated, and he turned on his tail and vanished into the bustling Damascus afternoon, promising to later return. He never did. Whoever the curious caller really was, he seemed determined to ensure his identity never became known after handing over his amazing treasures to Copeland.

Recognizing that, whatever the nature and subject of the material that had fallen so mysteriously into his lap, it was surely of some deep significance, Copeland quickly raced to the roof of the Embassy, along with two colleagues, and carefully unrolled the unique collection to photograph it. To the alarm of all three, however, bits and pieces of the old material began to flake and fragment as the wind suddenly picked up speed. Copeland could only stand and stare, helpless, as the disintegrating data floated like snowflakes down into the winding streets below. There was not a single moment to lose. Gathering his wits, Copeland quickly photographed as much of the remaining parchment as he conceivably could. He then personally delivered the developed 30 or so pictures and the original negatives to Roosevelt, who was working out of the American Embassy in Beirut at the time, and who, equally as intrigued as Copeland, promised to have it all checked out. The remains of the parchment, meanwhile, were dutifully placed in a drawer in Copeland's office for safe-keeping. And here's where the trail gets downright cold.

Copeland later heard a few Agency-originated whispers that the material represented a fragment of what ultimately became known as the Dead Sea Scrolls, and was specifically related to the Hebrew Bible's book of the Judean exile, Daniel. And, though Copeland learned that somewhere in officialdom the priceless text was the subject of deep analysis, no one ever fully confided in him what the CIA had discovered from studying his unique photographs. Nor did Copeland ever get an answer as to why he had been sought out in the first place by the enigmatic Egyptian who turned up so strangely on his doorstep on that fateful morning in the latter part of 1947. And there was more high-strangeness to come: The original material that Copeland was careful to secrete in a drawer in his office vanished, never to be seen again. Case closed? No, wide open. And it spilled over into yet another controversy: Those strange aerial objects—flying saucers—that firmly hit the world's stage in June 1947, only a few months before Miles Copeland's curious experience in Damascus.

SAUCERS AND SCROLLS

The Rise of the Saucers

On the afternoon of June 24, 1947, a pilot named Kenneth Arnold was diligently searching for an aircraft that had reportedly careened into the southwest side of Mt. Rainier, a large peak on Washington's huge Cascade Mountains. "I hadn't flown more than two or three minutes on my course when a bright flash reflected on my airplane," Arnold began after his unsuccessful search for the plane was over. "It startled me as I thought I was too close to some other aircraft. I looked every place in the sky and couldn't find where the reflection had come from until I looked to the left and the north of Mt. Rainier, where I observed a chain of nine peculiar looking aircraft flying from north to south at approximately 9,500 feet elevation and going, seemingly, in a definite direction of about 170 degrees" (Arnold, 1947).

Arnold added that the mysterious craft were closing in rapidly on the mountain, and he openly admitted to being baffled by their unusual shape and design. "I thought it was very peculiar that I couldn't find their tails," he said, "but assumed they were some type of jet plane. The more I observed these objects, the more upset I became, as I am accustomed and familiar with most all objects flying whether I am close to the ground or at higher altitudes. The chain of these saucer-like objects [was] at least five miles long. I felt confident after I would land there would be some explanation of what I saw [sic]" (Ibid.).

Only a little more than a week after Kenneth Arnold's life-changing experience, something very unusual plunged to earth in the deserts of Lincoln County, New Mexico, not far from the infamous town of Roswell. The event has been the subject of dozens of books, official studies undertaken by both the General Accounting Office and the U.S. Air Force, a plethora of television documentaries, a Hollywood movie called *Roswell*, and considerable media scrutiny. The admittedly odd saga has left in its wake a near-mountain of theories to explain the event, including a weather balloon, a *Project Mogul* balloon secretly utilized to monitor for Soviet atomic-bomb tests, an extraterrestrial spacecraft, some dark and dubious high-altitude-exposure experiment using Japanese prisoners of war, a near-catastrophic, atomic-bomb-based mishap, the crash of a V-2 rocket with shaved monkeys on board, and an accident involving an early aircraft secretly built by transplanted German scientists who had relocated to the United States following the end of World War II.

Whatever the exact nature of the device, it certainly seems to have been extraordinary in nature. Jesse A. Marcel, the intelligence officer for the 509th Bomb Group at Roswell Army Air Field in 1947, who personally saw, handled, and even collected some of the remains of the object at the crash site, the Foster Ranch, said of it years later: "The wreckage was scattered over an area about three-quarters of a mile long and several hundred feet wide. What is was we didn't know. We just picked up the fragments. [It] could not be bent or broken...or even dented by a sixteen-pound sledgehammer. [It was] almost weightless...like a metal with plastic properties" (Moore, 1982).

The Roswell event was born and the era of the flying saucer was ushered in—in spectacular style, one might very reasonably argue. And with the origins of the UFO puzzle now described, it's time to learn what on Earth, or, quite possibly, off of it, all this has to do with the U.S. government's interest in the Dead Sea Scrolls. For the answer to that conundrum we have to take a gigantic and dramatic leap from the heart of Damascus in 1947 to early-1990s California.

Deep Throat Discussions

In 1991, a man named Timothy Cooper, of Big Bear Lake, California, exploded onto the UFO research scene amid a storm of furious debate. This is not surprising, because Cooper brought with him to the ufological table a huge selection of very controversial data and official-looking documentation of a reportedly top-secret nature. Cooper claimed the priceless stash had been secretly provided to him by a number of *Deep Throat* like sources with personal knowledge of some of the U.S. government's most deeply guarded and troubling secrets relative to extraterrestrial visitation. The startling papers said to have been leaked to Cooper told of classified investigations into UFO activity and of crashed UFO incidents in the New Mexico desert in 1947. They also told of a powerful group of people buried deep within the U.S. government—from the CIA, the National Security Agency, the military, and a wealth of other agencies—tasked with studying, and hiding from the public and the media, the truth of the Roswell affair, as well as other sensational UFO events and alien-themed information. The secret group, supposedly, became known as MJ12 or Majestic 12.

One of the most interesting of all Cooper's sources was a man that Cooper initially referred to only as Bob. This particularly talkative source claimed to Cooper, in a face-to-face interview on September 9, 1990, that, while stationed at Holloman Air Force Base, New Mexico in 1948, he (Bob) had been exposed to a lengthy document on the crash of an incredibly advanced aircraft of unknown origins within the confines of the deeply sensitive White Sands Proving Ground in the previous year, 1947. Cooper later made available the cover-page of a document that he had acquired from yet another of his sources that was dated July 16, 1947. Titled *Air Accident Report on "Flying Disc" Aircraft Near the White Sands Proving Ground, New Mexico*, it bolstered the story of the crash of a UFO in New Mexico in the summer of 1947. Given that the White Sands Proving Ground—today called the White Sands Missile Range—was, and certainly still is, one of the United States's most secretive locales (it was here that captured Nazi scientists spent years working on

rocket- and missile-based programs in the immediate period after World War II), the document also reinforced
the image of Cooper cultivating distinctly interesting
sources of data within both the military and intelligence
communities.

The years passed by and Cooper, not surprisingly, became more and more visible within the UFO research
arena, as did the intricacies of his long and winding story
that unraveled at a near-exponential rate. In 1996, it was
revealed that Cooper's whistleblower source for the story of
the White Sands, New Mexico UFO crash—the mysterious
Bob—was actually none other than his very own father:
Harry B. Cooper, who had a lengthy and verifiable career in
the U.S. military.

As Cooper told it, his father chose to confide in him when
Harry saw Timothy reading the first published book on
the Roswell affair—*The Roswell Incident* by Charles Berlitz and William Moore, which surfaced in 1980. Not only
did Harry Cooper quietly, and noticeably guardedly, inform
his son that the Berlitz-Moore book had exposed the bare
bones of a very real and extraordinary event of a UFO nature, Harry added that he had held a position of some re-
sponsibility within the Reprographics Building at Holloman
and personally knew something of the very matter itself.
Harry Cooper continued that on one occasion in 1948, a
Colonel Paul Helmick—who was a former commanding officer with the Alamogordo Army Air Force, New Mexico—
arrived on-site with a document pouch locked to his wrist
and with two MPs ominously by his side, both sporting
machine guns. Clearly something of deep importance was
afoot.

Scrolls and saucers at White Sands.
(Copyright Nick Redfern.)

According to Harry Cooper, all of the on-duty personnel, aside from him, were told to leave the office, after which 10 copies of the document in question were laboriously made by Cooper, at the express and stern orders of Helmick. Also copied were a number of photographs contained within the report that allegedly showed a crashed UFO at a desert locale at White Sands in 1947. Unsurprisingly, Cooper was told if he knew what was good for him he should completely forget what he had just seen and, instead, just concentrate on being a good soldier for the rest of his career. Cooper most certainly *did* know what was good for him, and he did precisely as he was ordered—that is, anyway, until he finally chose to confide in his son decades later, possibly as a result of his conscience being unable to keep hidden such profound and monumental secrets any longer.

But there was something else that Timothy Cooper learned as a result of his exposure to the startling story of his own very father, and the intriguing collection of files provided to him by his secret band of whistleblowers of the cosmic kind. It was something startling. It was even something that had the potential to irreversibly shatter integral aspects of history and religion. And it led right back to the early days of the CIA and the Dead Sea Scrolls.

Scrolls in the Saucer

According to Timothy Cooper, the most sensational revelation related to the crash of the curious flying machine at the mountain-surrounded White Sands in 1947 was that within its wrecked confines nothing less than the remains of an incredibly old Hebrew Bible were carefully retrieved by the military operatives tasked with the recovery of the craft. His father had informed him that the near-priceless artifact was secretly provided to select, trusted scholars at Harvard who—expertly conversant in the Hebrew language back to its very earliest times—were tasked with trying to translate its complex text, which they were reportedly only partially successful at doing.

One of those who allegedly studied the material at Harvard was a Hebrew expert named William Foxwell Albright. Notably, of the Dead Sea Scrolls found at Qumran, Albright had told John C. Trever (of the Jerusalem-based American Schools of Oriental Research and the author of *The Untold Story of Qumran*) that they represented the "greatest manuscript discovery of modern times, certainly the greatest biblical find." Albright, whose published books include *The Archaeology of Palestine* and *The Biblical Period from Abraham to Ezra*, would have been one of the most ideal, and certainly one of the most enthused, people to get on board when it came to an analysis of the alleged White Sands discovery (Cook, 1994).

But, so Cooper was told, after years and years of studious, secret analysis, the staff at Harvard was still having big problems deciphering the text. So, by 1955, Cooper was informed, the ancient bible was placed in the hands of some of the nation's leading code-breakers and language experts at the National Security Agency (NSA), Fort Meade, Maryland, who were eagerly looking to take the investigation to its next level.

One of Cooper's sources—who went by a pseudonym, Thomas Cantwheel—informed him that "the Hebrew Bible was confirmed as the long-sought-after key to understanding extraterrestrial UFO sightings, and this information was shared with the Vatican as early as 1949." Moreover, Cooper added that his informants had advised him the manuscript found within the crashed UFO was written in a proto-Hebrew language. It was deemed by William F. Friedman (a renowned code-breaker who, in 1952, held the title of chief cryptologist at the NSA) and Lambros D. Callimahos (a colleague of, and an ultimate successor to, Friedman who wrote a number of UFO-themed papers for the NSA that are now available via the terms of the Freedom of Information Act) to be incredibly old and not at all easily understood or interpreted (Cantwheel, 1996).

But three things were certain: (1) that the translated parts of the ancient Bible found in New Mexico in 1947 dovetailed closely with certain data contained in the Dead Sea Scrolls, *also* uncovered in 1947, but on the other side of the world at Qumran; (2) that the book's pages held religion-challenging secrets suggesting that many early accounts of amazing miracles, of angelic manifestations, of demonic activity, of strange visions and dreams, and of apparitions in the skies of the Middle East had far more to do with the technologically based actions of highly advanced ancient aliens than they did with the supernatural realms of Heaven, Hell, God, and the Devil; and (3) that a significant amount of time was spent by U.S. officialdom analyzing data in the recovered Bible relative to the Book of Daniel.

This latter point is, in itself, particularly intriguing, because the Book of Daniel—which was reportedly referenced heavily in the material provided to CIA operative Miles Copeland in the fall of 1947 and which is also described in a number of the verifiable Dead Sea Scrolls—is replete with tales of Daniel's bizarre and unearthly visions and dreams. Many of them occurred during Daniel's time spent in Babylon at the court of the legendary king, Nebuchadnezzar II, who consulted Daniel on the nature and meaning of his own dreams and nightmares.

The stark conclusion of senior elements in the NSA, therefore, was that the cornerstones of worldwide religion were very possibly nothing less than the distorted tales of early visitations from enigmatic travelers borne within the depths of far-away galaxies, and that this was somehow in evidence in the material on the legends of Daniel as found in the flying saucer recovered from White Sands. Little wonder, then, that the story—and its links to the Dead Sea Scrolls—was deemed one that could never, *ever*, be told to the public at large.

Secret Truths vs. Outrageous Fantasy

The big question that all of the previous questions beg is: How much of this extraordinary and undeniably controversial data can be verified? Can *any* of it be verified?

Certainly, no one disputes the existence of the Dead Sea Scrolls; they are, after all, a matter of historical fact. Likewise, Miles Copeland—who died in 1991—spoke on the record and candidly on several occasions about his exposure to what seemed to have been a portion of the Dead Sea Scrolls, and confirmed this did occur during his tenure with the CIA in Damascus, and that the Agency most certainly took an interest in the scrolls. And there is no doubt that the entire affair as related by Copeland was one of mystery, of a clandestine visitor, of missing papers, and of unique photographs that have still yet to surface out of the impenetrable archives of the CIA. Yes, Kenneth Arnold did experience something strange in the skies of Washington State in 1947. And some form of flying machine, the nature and origin of which apparently still troubles the U.S. government to this very day, most assuredly did crash to earth near Roswell, New Mexico, only a week or so after Arnold's experience.

But what are we to make of Timothy Cooper's amazing tale linking crashed Flying Saucers to the Dead Sea Scrolls? As controversial as Timothy Cooper's story most certainly is, in 2004 I personally secured copies of his father's official military records from the National Personnel Records Center (NPRC) in St. Louis, Missouri. They indicated Harry Cooper served in the Marine Corps from September 26, 1941 to December 24, 1945, and in the Air Force from October 11, 1947 to July 13, 1960. During the latter service, Cooper *was* stationed at Holloman, New Mexico, in 1948, and later at March Air Force Base, California, and Wiesbaden Air Base, Germany, which was his last tour of duty. Harry B. Cooper died on September 2, 2000, and his remains are buried in Riverside National Cemetery, California.

Was Cooper exposed to real informatior documentation? Was it comprised of nothin; ceit and lies, mixed in with a very liberal do.. .. .., ... order to confuse and flummox Cooper while engaged in his UFO studies? Did he, as some believe, fake it all himself? Or, might Cooper have been given wholly real data, but data presented in a fashion that would guarantee him no backlash from the U.S. government if he decided to go public with the astounding story? Interestingly enough, Cooper's very own sources claimed it was precisely the latter scenario that was correct.

On February 29, 1996, Cooper received a last, memorable letter from the shadowy Thomas Cantwheel. Dated exactly one week previously, it began in dramatic, eye-catching style: "Dear Mr. Cooper: By the time this letter reaches you, I will have left this world. I have cancer and don't have much time." In that same letter, Cantwheel divulged yet more data on what he claimed had motivated him to speak with Cooper. He also revealed one particular startling fact: that the material he had provided to Cooper did *not* represent genuine, official documentation at all. It was not faked, either, Cantwheel assured Cooper. Rather, the documents were, as Cantwheel much preferred the term, "constructs" (Cooper, 1996).

In his final missive to Cooper, Cantwheel explained further what he meant by "constructs": "There are many things to tell you about the 1947 New Mexico discoveries that I was personally involved with, but, the grave beckons me most earnestly and will not wait any longer. In regards to the documents, I must assume that you have had them investigated by the so-called 'experts' by now and have determined that some were obvious fakes. Sorry about that. The others were copies and Xeroxed from originals. These came from my personal files" (Ibid.).

The documents were not fakes designed to deceive Cooper, however, assured Cantwheel. They were quite the opposite, and directly intended to help Cooper in his quest for the truth behind the UFO puzzle: "As for the manner in which you received them, it was necessary to construct them in a way so as to protect you from criminal prosecution. But, I assure you that the names, dates, and places are valid. I think I provided you with enough leads to help you find valuable information that can be found in any library. I hope you will not think too ill of me for leading you on for so long. I believe that in good time, the intelligence community will be forced to open up more UFO intelligence files to the public. UFOs will not go away, and will only increase in intensity" (Ibid.).

That the data provided to Cooper may have included certain distortions to try to protect him from prosecution by the U.S. government if matters escalated, might explain why, in 1986, a UFO researcher named William Steinman published a very similar story about an ancient parchment being found in a crashed UFO. Steinman's insider sources, however, stated that the crash had occurred in 1948, not 1947. And the location was not the White Sands Proving Ground, as Cooper had been advised, but on a mesa just outside the small New Mexican town of Aztec, which is located in the northern part of the state. Maybe Steinman himself was fed a similar body of distorted data to that of Cooper. We may never really know, except for one thing: Both Steinman and Cooper appeared to have been the recipients of fairly extensive and detailed data on crashed UFOs and the Dead Sea Scrolls that someone in officialdom sorely wanted to get into the public domain. The pseudonymous Thomas Cantwheel—like each and every one of Cooper's informants—faded away into the shadowy darkness from which he originally surfaced.

SECRETS OF
THE ARK

Getting Into Deep Waters

Within the pages of the Holy Bible, specifically in the Book of Genesis, we are told that: "God looked upon the earth, and, behold, it was corrupt; for all flesh had corrupted his way upon the earth. And God said unto Noah, The end of all flesh is come before me; for the earth is filled with violence through them; and, behold, I will destroy them with the earth" (Genesis 6:12–13).

Not quite everyone was due to be obliterated, however. So the old legend goes: God had major, historic plans in store for Noah, who the Bible describes as being the grandson of Methuselah, the oldest person ever referenced within the pages of the book. Noah was instructed by God to "make thee an Ark of gopher wood; rooms shalt thou make in the Ark, and shalt pitch it within and without with pitch. And this is the fashion which thou shalt make it of: The length of the Ark shall be three hundred cubits, the breadth of it fifty cubits, and the height of it thirty cubits. A window shalt thou make to the Ark, and in a cubit shalt thou finish it above; and the door of the Ark shalt thou set in the side thereof; with lower, second, and third stories shalt thou make it" (Genesis 6:14–16).

The reasoning behind God's decision to have Noah construct the huge, mighty Ark became terrifyingly clear as matters quickly advanced. In what we are advised were God's own words, he thundered: "And, behold, I, even I, do bring a flood of waters upon the earth, to destroy all flesh, wherein is the breath of life, from under heaven; and every thing that is in the earth shall die" (Genesis 6:17).

Noah, however, was due to be spared God's planet-wide pummeling and deluge-style wrath: "But with thee will I establish my covenant; and thou shalt come into the Ark, thou, and thy sons, and thy wife, and thy sons' wives with thee. And of every living thing of all flesh, two of every sort shalt thou bring into the Ark, to keep them alive with thee; they shall be male and female. Of fowls after their kind, and of cattle after their kind, of every creeping thing of the earth after his kind, two of every sort shall come unto thee, to keep them alive. And take thou unto thee of all food that is eaten, and thou shalt gather it to thee; and it shall be for food for thee, and for them" (Genesis 6:19–21).

Noah prepares to survive the Flood.
(Edward Hicks, 1846.)

Thus was created the now-world-famous story of Noah's
Ark, which culminated in the man himself, his family, and
his huge menagerie of animals surviving in the sturdy confines of the Ark for 40 cataclysmic days and nights, after
which the giant ship is said to have come to rest when the
wild and turbulent waters did likewise. The story is without doubt a controversial one, particularly so when one
takes into consideration that even among religious scholars there is significant dissent and disagreement regarding the origins and nature of the tale, and even on the
ultimate resting place of Noah's Ark that most Christians,

today, accept as being somewhere high on the cold and treacherous slopes of Mt. Ararat, Turkey.

The Other Floods

It is worth noting that flood legends exist within the history, folklore, and mythologies of numerous, diverse cultures all around the world; they are far from being exclusive to Christian teachings or even to Mt. Ararat and its immediate surroundings. As evidence of this, tales of gigantic floods overwhelming and pulverizing the planet in distant times have surfaced from nations as diverse as Wales, Sweden, Denmark, Norway, Finland, Greece, Korea, China, Argentina, Bolivia, Peru, and also among a whole variety of Native American Indian tribes. And the stories are astonishingly, and profoundly, very similar in nature.

Hindu teachings tell of the powerful Manu, the first Brahman king said to have ruled our planet, who salvaged the human race from the clutches of an all-destructive flood during the early years of human civilization. In this story, however, rather than being Mt. Ararat, the touch-down point for the huge ship that Manu (not Noah) constructed was the Malaya Mountains, which today are known as the Western Ghats, a large range located on the west side of India.

The Sumerian *Epic of Gilgamesh*—which is most extensively described on a dozen large tablets from the library of an Assyrian king, Ashurbanipal, who reigned in the seventh century BC—also has its very own cataclysmic flood legend. The tablets date from approximately 650 BC, but they tell a story that in all likelihood extends much, *much* further into the past. Frank Lorey says of the tablets that they contain "little of value for Christians," because they focus upon "typical polytheistic myths associated with the pagan peoples of the times" (Lorey, 2011).

Nevertheless, the clear similarities to the legend of Noah's Ark are as deep as they are undeniable. In *Gilgamesh*, a man named Utnapishtim builds a huge boat, aboard which he, his family, and numerous animals survive a catastrophic global flood. Sound familiar? The Native Americans have their own flood story, too. They believe that when the human race lost favor with Gitche Manitou (a Native American creator figure, whose name can be spelled in a variety of ways, depending upon the tribe) it was punished by huge floods that wiped out much of life on Earth, both human and animal.

The flood tales, therefore, do seem to have some basis in historical reality. Cultural beliefs, localized traditions, and religious preferences and prejudices, however, have almost certainly helped to ensure that separating reality from fiction, and exaggeration from distorted oral tradition passed down across the centuries, is a monumentally problematic task. But that there *were* huge floods in times past—and possibly ones that had devastating and lasting effects upon major land masses and entire populations—is not just the stuff of fairy tales. It's actually the stuff of nightmarish reality.

In 1997, Walter Clarkson Pitman III, a professor emeritus and a geophysicist at Columbia University, and a geologist named William Ryan offered the theory that the story of the biblical deluge was born, possibly as early as 5,600 BC, out of a significantly sized flooding of the Black Sea, which, in part, borders Turkey, home to Mt. Ararat. Then there are the findings of Bruce Masse, an environmental archaeologist of the Los Alamos National Laboratory, who theorized that around 5,000 years ago a huge comet may have impacted—with devastating force—off the coast of Madagascar, provoking gigantic tidal waves, death on a near-unimaginable and obscene scale, and the development of the very types of flood legends we have today. That other such similar events may have occurred in additional parts of the world millennia ago may have helped nurture similar accounts of huge floods, too. But, there is one very significant thing that makes the story of Noah's Ark stand out from all of the other flood legends on record: the deep, secret interest that the U.S. government has taken in the controversy.

The Ark on Film

On the morning of June 17, 1949, a United States Air Force crew quietly took to the skies from a military base in Europe on a clandestine and dicey mission. The plan was to photograph what American Intelligence learned was a disturbing build-up in Soviet military facilities and weapons on land extremely close to the border of Turkey. The crew's secret flight was destined to take it over the huge, near-17,000-foot-high, snow-covered Mt. Ararat—something that turned out to be a life-changing, historic experience for the men aboard the plane and that has secretly occupied the finest minds of the Pentagon, the CIA, the military, and a host of other intelligence-gathering agencies ever since.

When the crew reached a height of around 14,000 feet, the chief photographer aboard the aircraft was amazed to see what appeared to be a gargantuan, intelligently designed craft of some sort—seemingly no less than 500 feet in length, and possibly even as long as 600 feet—partially protruding from the thick ice that was dominating Mt. Ararat's southwest face. The crew, as dumbfounded as they were excited, hastily maneuvered the aircraft in a concerted effort to secure a better viewing of the extraordinary object, which they most certainly did. The pilot skillfully, albeit tentatively, closed in on it, while the rest of the men scrambled and craned for a closer look. As they did so, one of them shouted that he could see what looked like a very similar and equally huge object, not too far away, situated on Mt. Ararat's western side.

Incredibly, as the pilot then turned the plane and focused his attention on this second puzzle, all aboard could see that it resembled the wing of an aircraft that had become trapped within the thick ice and snow. But, if it *was* the wing of an air-craft, then it most certainly belonged to no ordinary plane. Size-wise it easily eclipsed anything that either the Americans or the Russians were flying at the time. The wing, if that is what it really was, was *huge*. Photographs were quickly taken and, unsurprisingly, soon thereafter received the ominous stamp of secrecy and vanished, for decades, into the shadowy and Machiavellian heart of officialdom. The U.S. government's secret study of Noah's Ark and the mountain of mystery had just begun. But it would not be too long before there were fur-ther, extraordinary developments in the saga.

Three years later, a man named Bill Todd, who was serv-ing with the U.S. military in Turkey at the time, was also witness to a gigantic object on Mt. Ararat that was partially eclipsed by snow and ice. Somewhat tellingly, Todd said the vast conundrum reminded him of a large, rectangu-lar-shaped, slate-colored ship. Then, there is the story of Lieutenant Colonel Robert Livingston. In 1954, Livingston was on a temporary posting to Wright-Patterson Air Force Base, Ohio, in a field office of the Topographic Engineering Center that had its primary base of operations at Fort Belvoir, Virginia. Livingston, who worked at Fort Belvoir from 1948 to 1972—having ultimately retired as the Chief of Field Office—was into his 80s and well past retirement when he revealed how, at Wright-Patterson one morning in 1954, an Air Force captain unknown to him brought into the office a solitary photograph that had reportedly been supplied by a U.S. attaché at the Turkish Embassy and that had been secured by the crew of an American military reconnaissance aircraft.

Livingston recalled that the photograph clearly showed an elongated rectangular object that had a dark outline and appeared to be underneath a sheet of ice. He and his team were ordered by the captain to make an evaluation of the extraordinary dimensions of the strange formation, which they did, after approximately an hour of studying the picture. The captain then retrieved the photograph, thanked the men, and went on his way—never to be seen again.

Twelve months later, in 1955, now-declassified CIA files reveal that a French adventurer, one Fernand Navarra, came across a sizeable piece of very old wood, which had clearly been fashioned by human hand, relatively close to one of the two sites photographed by the U.S. Air Force back in 1949. Deeply significant is the fact that the Air Force's photographs of 1949 were still kept behind closed doors in 1955, which means that Navarra's discovery of the priceless wooden artifact was made unknowingly, and wholly independently, of the Air Force's findings, thus reinforcing the idea that some form of ancient craft really *was* present in that specific area.

Then there is the noteworthy testimony of Captain Gregor Schwinghammer. It was at some point in the latter part of the 1950s, while stationed in Adana, Turkey, with the U.S. Air Force, that Schwinghammer was also lucky enough to see what may well have been the remains of Noah's incredible feat of nautical engineering. It looked, he recalled, like a huge rectangular barge. Schwinghammer added that, to his personal knowledge, on at least one occasion a U-2 spy-plane had been utilized to secure close-up photographs of the UFO, the unidentified frozen object. They were pictures that indicated the Ark had slid down the mountain and become banked at some point in the past.

Also during the late 1950s, the British equivalent of the CIA, MI6, secretly shared with American Intelligence its very own files on Noah's Ark. The bulk of the material provided to the CIA focused upon an attempt by the Nazis to locate the remains of Noah's Ark from mid-1944 to early-1945. MI6 files do not explain exactly *why* the Nazis were so keen to uncover the truth about the Ark; however, that a concerted, secret effort was underway to find it was not a matter of doubt. According to MI6's informants in Turkey, the Nazis sought to obtain photographs of the area where the Ark could reportedly be found and launched at least two balloon-based missions over Mt. Ararat to try to achieve that precise goal. The attempts were apparently unsuccessful, but they did serve to help convince U.S. authorities of the late-1950s that, if the Germans had been searching for the Ark more than a decade earlier, and the Brits were taking secret note too, then there was probably something up there that was well worth finding.

Smithsonian Secrets

The controversial notion that the Washington, D.C.–based Smithsonian Institution might be hiding profound and secret archeological data on Noah's Ark sounds like the perfect plot for the next *Indiana Jones* movie—Harrison Ford-willing, of course. But, such a precise and astonishing claim *has* been made. And it has nothing, in the slightest, to do with the world of on-screen Hollywood fiction. It came from David Duckworth, who, in the latter part of 1968, was working at the Smithsonian. One day several wooden crates, reportedly containing a number of old tools and pieces of ancient timber that attracted deep interest, and provoked major gossip, on the part of the employees, were quietly and carefully brought on-site.

Possibly of relevance to the documentation on the Nazi-hunt for the Ark that MI6 shared with the CIA in the latter part of the 1950s, Duckworth recalled that, along with the cargo, were a number of photographs of Mt. Ararat, reportedly secured via balloon, which revealed a boat-type object semi-obscured by thick ice. Not only that: Duckworth asked a few questions of his colleagues and was told that the curious items brought to the Smithsonian were from Noah's Ark. Less than a week later, however, the lid of secrecy came crashing down, just like those old flood-driven waves of times long past. Employees were told to say no more about the priceless find, and all of the evidence was carefully gathered together and shipped away to destinations unknown. That was not quite the end of the story, however.

Despite the clear warning not to talk to anyone, Duckworth failed to remain silent, and parts of his story ultimately surfaced within the pages of Violet Cummings's 1982 book, *Has Anyone Really Seen Noah's Ark?* Interestingly, although Cummings's book was published many years after Duckworth's experience at the Smithsonian took place, evidently someone was still clandestinely watching him, or was at least monitoring any and all developments in the Ark saga. Or, maybe, it was a combination of both. As evidence of this, it didn't take long at all before the FBI was making Duckworth's life a misery, strongly suggesting, in a face-to-face interview, that it would be very unwise to say any more about his 1960s memories of the Ark variety. For the most part, Duckworth did not. But as the 1960s came to a close, and as a new decade dawned, government interest in Noah's Ark continued, behind closed doors and at a secret, steady pace.

ARARAT AND
THE AGENCY

Secret "Arkives"

Without doubt, one of the most significant contributions to the Noah's Ark controversy is a batch of official
documentation on the matter that, under the terms of
the Freedom of Information Act, has surfaced from the
archives of the CIA. Granted, the papers contain no undeniable smoking gun, or photos of pieces of old and decaying
wood, but, collectively, they are still an important, integral,
and fascinating part of the overall story. Although there is,
as we have already seen, a wealth of on-the-record testimony
strongly demonstrating deep military and government
interest in the story of Noah's Ark from the late 1940s to

the end of the 1960s, the CIA's own records are totally lacking in any files or documents from this particular era. In fact, the material that the CIA has so far chosen to release into the public domain dates solely from the early 1970s onward. Quite understandably, this has inevitably led to allegations that the most interesting and earlier data still remains hidden behind closed doors—a theory that, as we shall see, may very well possess some real merit.

CIA memoranda reveals that on May 13, 1973, CIA Director William Colby contacted the Agency's Directorate of Science and Technology, and also informed Sayre Stevens, a former deputy director of intelligence, that Lt. Col. Walter Brown of the U.S. Air Force Academy had recently made inquiries to determine if any evidence of the existence of Noah's Ark had been found on CIA-originated photographs of Mt. Ararat. Brown, it seems, had heard whispers of *something*. We do not know what went on behind the scenes at the CIA's Langley, Virginia, headquarters, but Brown was quickly told that although aerial photography of the mountain *had* been obtained—specifically on September 10, 1957 by the pilot of a U-2 plane—it showed nothing mysterious, or anything of any real substance in the slightest. That didn't prevent the CIA from flatly refusing to release, declassify, or even show the claimed innocuous photos to Brown, however.

If the pictures really *did* just show a lot of rock, ice, snow, and not much else, one is inevitably forced to ask a few important questions: Why was there an overwhelming desire to keep the imagery safely behind lock and key? Where was the harm in releasing photos of a Turkish mountain? And, surely declassifying the pictures would have put to rest the conspiracy theories that the CIA knew far more than it was publicly willing to tell. Whatever the truth behind this matter, it's worth noting that the CIA's admittance that a U-2 spy-plane had been employed to photograph Mt. Ararat in the 1950s accords very well with the testimony of Captain Gregor Schwinghammer. He had also made such a specific claim, but his words starkly contrasted with those of the CIA when he maintained that the U-2 imagery most certainly *did* show evidence of an Ark-like structure on the mountain.

The controversial Ararat Anomaly.
(Copyright U.S. Air Force.)

Congressional Inquiries

CIA files note that a little more than a year later, on August 6, 1974, Congressman Bob Wilson approached the Agency and inquired if a Dr. John Morris, the son of Dr. Henry Morris, and the then-head of the Institution of Creation Research of San Diego, California, could have access to certain photographs of Mt. Ararat that might finally resolve the controversy surrounding the reality, or otherwise, of Noah's Ark. A brief, but illuminating reply came from Angus Theurmer, who was the CIA's press spokesperson at the time. Possibly recognizing that he was dealing with a member of government (Congressman Wilson) who had some apparent knowledge of official interest in the controversy surrounding Mt. Ararat and what might possibly be resting on its snowy surface, Theurmer took careful steps and tactfully admitted to the congressman that, with respect to Noah's Ark, yes: The CIA *had* addressed this matter in some detail. He added, however, that the Agency was unable to provide any information or help whatsoever. Or, for all intents and purposes: Go away. Congressman Wilson, however, did not go away.

On January 30, 1975, Dr. John Morris yet again wrote to Wilson and informed him that further sources had revealed to him that aerial photos of the Ark had apparently been taken as late as 1974, specifically by U.S. Intelligence, no less. Moreover, Morris advised the congressman that he had heard the photos had been classified by officialdom. Precisely how Morris knew all of this remains tantalizingly unknown to this very day, but it turns out that he was right on target. After Wilson approached the CIA once more, documentation shows, both he and Morris were told that, yes, the pictures did exist. But, no, they could not be made available under any circumstances whatsoever. That written confirmation was received to the effect that classified photos of Mt. Ararat were in evidence, however, was certainly a small step in the right direction.

Book-Watching

The next revelation in the CIA file makes an absolute mockery of the idea that government personnel were largely uninterested in the saga of Noah's Ark. From March 27, 1975 to April 5, 1975, the previously referred to Fernand Navarra was busy publicizing his 1974 book, *Noah's Ark: I Touched It,* at a booth located at the Washington, D.C.–based Iverson Mall. And a key piece of evidence was on show, too: It was nothing less than a wooden fragment that Navarra believed was an actual piece of the Ark that had been smuggled back to the United States in a situation worthy of James Bond, 007, himself.

Rather intriguingly, CIA records note that several analysts from the Agency's National Photographic Interpretation Center (NPIC) visited the display without giving away their true identities to Navarra, in an effort to learn more about what the CIA described in summaries of the relevant 1975-era papers as "the Ark problem." In light of this thought-provoking quote, one might be very inclined to ask a particularly important question: If the CIA never found Noah's Ark, and the photos of Mt. Ararat showed nothing unusual, then why was there even a "problem" in the first place? And what was the specific nature of that same mysterious "problem"? (Central Intelligence Agency, 1982). Questions certainly abound. Definitive answers to those questions certainly do not.

It was not only the book of Fernand Navarra in which the CIA was taking a secret interest. Agency analysts also spent time carefully reviewing Thomas Nelson's *The Ark of Ararat* that was published in July 1975. They noted for the record that Nelson had heard and (to the CIA's complete and utter chagrin) had published the story of its classified photos of Mt. Ararat and the attendant Ark rumors. Three months later, the CIA sat up and took notice when a group called the Holy Ground Mission, which was based out of Frankston, Texas, started circulating a photograph that had been taken by one of their staff on an expedition to Mt. Ararat in 1974. The picture, believed the Holy Ground Mission, reportedly showed nothing less than the remains of the ancient Ark. When approached for comment by Ark enthusiasts, the CIA totally blew them off.

The Astronaut and the Ark

Matters became even more controversial in February 1982, when James B. Irwin (who was the pilot of NASA's *Apollo 15* Lunar Module and one of the handful of people to have ever walked on the surface of the Moon) telephoned, quite out of the blue and at his home, a former employee of the CIA's National Photographic Interpretation Center (NPIC), Dino A. Brugioni. Irwin, evidently aware that the NPIC and Brugioni had some involvement in the Ark issue, inquired about the status of, and access to, the photographs of Mt. Ararat and of the huge, mysterious boat, too. This should not be considered at all surprising: Beginning in 1973, Irwin personally led a number of ambitious expeditions to Mt. Ararat in search of the Ark that, unfortunately, were brought to a halt in 1982, when he was badly injured while navigating the treacherous, imposing mountain.

Brugioni, placed on the spot by Irwin's unannounced call, gave a quick and decisive reply: The CIA never found any evidence for the existence of Noah's Ark. As will become apparent shortly, Brugioni's words, though not at all deceptive, only added to the controversy.

There is then a glaring gap of 10 years in the files the CIA has seen fit to release on Noah's Ark. In 1992, an Ark enthusiast named Charles P. Aaron contacted the Agency, noting that he had the support of *Apollo* astronaut Irwin and a number of U.S. senators, and wanted to know if the CIA would be willing to help his group—called the Tsirah Corporation—find the Ark once and for all. After a bit of internal debate on the matter, the CIA politely declined to do so, but might just as well have said, "Hell, no!" Of far greater interest to Agency personnel, however, was Aaron's revelation— possibly a deeply *unwise* revelation—that insider sources had informed him that elements of the U.S. government had secretly developed photographic technology capable of penetrating through thick sheets of ice. Interested CIA staff sent memos back and forth discussing and debating whether or not there was any truth to this alleged technology, but ultimately denied to Aaron any and all knowledge of it.

Twelve months later, a CIA employee, whose name has been carefully excised from the declassified documentation, provided the director of Central Intelligence with an update on the CIA's then-current stance with respect to the Noah's Ark controversy. The same employee made a thought-provoking aside concerning how, and under what particular circumstances, an unnamed television production company had then recently been denied access to certain "imagery of Noah's Ark" held by the CIA. Note that the reference was not to Mt. Ararat, or even to some anomalous, undetermined blob on the side of the mountain, but specifically to "imagery of Noah's Ark" (Central Intelligence Agency, 1993). Was this an innocent, poorly worded phrase? Or might it have been a reference to something far more provocative? If anyone inside the CIA knows, they are most certainly not saying anything on the outside.

An equally notable statement came tumbling out of the CIA's archives in 2006, when a February 7, 1994 memo that originated with the Agency's Office of the Deputy Director for Science and Technology and that was dispatched to the CIA director, R. James Woolsey, was declassified. It stated that the CIA had "no efforts currently underway to conduct additional searches for Noah's Ark in the Mt. Ararat region." Even the most vociferous skeptic of the Ark affair will be forced to admit that any reference to *additional* searches" can mean only one thing: At some point in its past, the CIA *did* search for the Ark of Noah (Central Intelligence Agency, 1994).

The Mystery of the Mountain Continues

On March 14, 1995, as a result of the specific and persistent digging of Professor Porcher Taylor III of the University of Richmond, whose interest in the Ark story dated back to his time as a cadet at West Point in 1973, the Defense Intelligence Agency (DIA) took many Ark researchers by complete surprise when it declassified one of the legendary photographs of Mt. Ararat taken by the U.S. Air Force back in 1949. Possibly recognizing, quite correctly and very astutely, that the release of the photograph would likely lead to big waves within both the media and Ark-hunting circles, the DIA quickly and decisively chose to play down its significance and said: "The anomaly is located along an unstable precipice near the edge of the permanent glacial ice cap atop Mt. Ararat. The accumulated ice and snow along the precipice obviously fall down the side of the mountain at frequent intervals, often leaving long linear facades. It appears that the anomaly is one of these linear facades" (Defense Intelligence Agency, 1995).

When the DIA was forced to declassify even more of the imagery secured by the Air Force back in 1949, people really began to sit up and take notice. A naval engineer named Peter Hsu offered his opinion that the anomaly in the photographs might very well have been fashioned by human hand. Moreover, Taylor was contacted by a source who had secretly studied aerial imagery of the alleged Ark for the CIA in 1959–1960, and opined that whatever the nature of the object on the photos provided by the DIA in 1995, it was simply way too linear to have been created naturally, and seemed to be partially buried under the ice, which is something that many others who studied such photographic evidence, including Lt. Col. Robert Livingston, had also noted.

Recall that back in February 1982, Dino Brugioni, of the CIA's National Photographic Interpretation Center, was put on the spot by *Apollo* astronaut James Irwin, and denied that the CIA had any evidence that Noah's Ark had ever been found on Mt. Ararat. Well, in 1997, two years after the Defense Intelligence Agency released the Air Force's photos of 1949, Brugioni slightly modified his earlier position. When the Yom Kippur War erupted in October 1973, a CIA satellite in the area that was secretly spying on the escalating conflict was utilized to obtain new imagery of Mt. Ararat, as well as of the curious anomaly. Fifteen years after his brief conversation with James Irwin, and when stories of the Ark and officialdom were tumbling out, Brugioni admitted seeing those photographs from 1973. And although he was still as adamant as ever that he never concluded they definitively showed the Ark of Noah, Brugioni admitted they did at least reveal the presence of *something* on the mountain.

A second intelligence asset came forward in this same period, stating that at least one of the images showed what seemed to be gigantic beams of wood protruding from the dense ice and snow. Even George Alexander Carver Jr., who served under no less than three CIA directors, and who spent more than a quarter of a century in government, cagily admitted that, based on his evaluation of the 1973 photos, the Ark controversy was one that should be studied more closely.

But why, exactly, were the U.S. government, the Pentagon, and the Intelligence community of the 1950s–1990s so deeply, and secretly, interested in the possibility that Noah's Ark really had come to rest high on the freezing, precarious slopes of Mt. Ararat all those years ago? After all, even if the Ark *was* real, wouldn't its discovery and analysis have just been a matter for historians, archeologists, and the Church, rather than the secret-agents of American Intelligence? Yes, certainly, if the Ark was just an old, decaying boat. But, what if the Ark *wasn't* just a huge, wooden ship build thousands of years ago? Might it actually have been something far more incredible—perhaps something quite literally out of this world? It may not be entirely coincidental that, throughout the same time the Pentagon and the CIA were taking close notice of what was happening on Mt. Ararat, other agencies of the government and the military were busily at work, secretly addressing the issue of whether or not Noah's Ark might have had far more to do with the activities of space-faring extra-terrestrials than it did with God.

MOON DUST ON
THE MOUNTAIN

An Alien Ark

Originally a resident of Jefferson County, Ohio, but someone who ultimately gravitated to the far harsher climes of the California desert, George Wellington Van Tassel claimed decades of encounters with very human-appearing aliens that allegedly began in the summer of 1953 near his Yucca Valley home. The notable details of Van Tassel's alleged encounter, specifically of August 1953, were described for none other than legendary FBI director J. Edgar Hoover in a formerly classified report of November 16, 1954. It was in the early hours of that morning Hoover was told in secret memoranda that Van Tassel and his wife were camping in a desert location near Landers, California (known to one and all in the area as *Giant Rock*, as a result of a huge, ancient rock that to this day dominates the desert landscape) when something truly sensational and other-worldly was said to have occurred.

According to FBI records, Van Tassel was visited by an honest-to-goodness extra-terrestrial dressed in an outfit very reminiscent of that of a U.S. Air Force fighter pilot. The alien entity proceeded to invite the shocked Van Tassel to take a quick tour of his UFO, which had reportedly touched down near the huge rock only minutes earlier. Van Tassel earnestly told a pair of FBI special agents that visited his home in 1954 the vehicle in question was shaped somewhat like a bell and was more than 30 feet in diameter. It was no normal aircraft, then. As for the aliens themselves, Van Tassel said they conversed only via psychic means: telepathy. Their specific purpose for visiting the Earth, he was advised, was to carefully warn humankind that the ever-growing atomic arsenals of the superpowers posed a direct and catastrophic threat to the future of all life on Earth. Unless the human race changed its ways, Van Tassel was warned, our world would soon be destroyed by our own hands.

Galvanized and spurred on by the words of warning and wisdom from his alien visitors, Van Tassel then went out and preached the gospel of E.T. to just about anyone and everyone who would listen to him. And plenty did listen, too: From 1954 onward, Van Tassel elected to hold yearly flying saucer–themed conferences out at Landers, which, at their height in the mid-1950s, attracted audience numbers of an impressive five-figure range. But what really caught the attention of the FBI were Van Tassel's assertions that Christianity was borne out of alien visitation—ancient astronauts, as they have become famously known—and his views on our old friend, Noah, and his mysterious and massive Ark.

On April 17, 1960, Van Tassel gave a lengthy speech at the Phipps Auditorium in Denver, Colorado, having been invited to do so by the local Denver Unidentified Flying Objects Investigative Society. To ensure that the lecture was a resounding success, the society took out a great deal of advertising time on Denver-based radio stations that caught the attention of the city's FBI office, which subsequently directed a special agent to clandestinely attend and report back the details of Van Tassel's speech. Relevant extracts read as follows: "The program consisted of a 45-minute movie which included several shots of things purported to be flying saucers, and then a number of interviews with people from all walks of life regarding sightings they had made of such unidentified flying objects. After the movie George W. Van Tassel gave a lecture which was more of a religious-economics lecture than one of unidentified flying objects (Federal Bureau of Investigation, 1960).

It was this particular "religious-economics" aspect of the speech that made J. Edgar Hoover's finest sit up and take careful notice. The special agent in attendance recorded, in a lengthy report prepared two days later, that: "The major part of [Van Tassel's] lecture was devoted to explaining the occurrences in the Bible as they related to the space people. He said that in the beginning of the world the space people came to the earth and left animals here. These were the prehistoric animals which existed at a body temperature of 105 degrees; however a polar tilt occurred whereby the poles shifted and the tropical climates became covered with ice and vice-versa" (Ibid.).

The FBI agent secretly in attendance said Van Tassel elaborated that to ensure life on Earth continued following the Ice Age, alien visitors populated our planet with other species of animal, and it was this specific action that led to the direct creation of the legend of Noah's Ark. Van Tassel explained further, however, that millennia after this ambitious, mega-scale re-seeding of our planet took place, the aliens were forced to hastily return, yet again, and save whole swathes of the human and animal populations when a worldwide flood, provoked by a further, unanticipated planetary tilt, wrought untold havoc, disaster, and destruction on a massive scale. The result was that yet another layer was added to the already-complicated story of the Ark of Noah.

On the issue of other biblical tales and stories, Van Tassel continued that directly after the aforementioned first polar tilt, aliens from a faraway world established a male-only colony on Earth, intending to bring the females at a later date on what were termed "supply ships." This, Van Tassel said, and the FBI noted, was "reflected in Adam not having a wife. Adam was not an individual but a race of men." Further, according to the FBI's now-declassified records: "[Van Tassel] said that this race then intermarried with 'intelligent, upright walking animals,' which race was EVE [sic]. Then when the space people came back in the supply ships they saw what had happened and did not land; but ever since due to the origin of ADAM, they have watched over the people on Earth" (Ibid.).

Part of that same process of secret surveillance, asserted Van Tassel, and as the FBI faithfully recorded, included the aliens ensuring that the human race was taught certain rules, regulations, and morals as part of a concerted, purposeful effort to control and manipulate us. Those same rules, regulations, and morals, claimed Van Tassel, were in actuality nothing less than the legendary Ten Commandments, as provided to Moses on Mount Sinai by God. Van Tassel's bold assertion was that the Ten Commandments had nothing to do with any God whatsoever, Christian or otherwise. Rather, he maintained, the Commandments were actually "the laws of the space-people." Also borne of the very same space-people, Van Tassel told the audience at the Phipps Auditorium, was Jesus Christ himself, who Van Tassel described as being the product of Mary, "a space person sent here already pregnant in order to show the earth people the proper way to live" (Ibid.).

Though it is certainly true that George Van Tassel was a highly controversial character, the FBI took a great deal of interest in the man and his claims concerning UFOs, the Holy Bible, Noah's Ark, and the origins of Christianity. As evidence of this, his FBI file ran to almost 400 pages, spanned 15 years, and was copied *in full* to elements of both the CIA and the National Security Agency. More significantly, as far as can be presently determined at least, this was the first documented occasion upon which elements of the U.S. Intelligence community took extensive interest in the claims of someone who asserted Noah's Ark was somehow linked with the work of ancient extra-terrestrials that visited the Earth thousands of years ago. It was most certainly not to be the last time, however.

Moon Dust Mysteries

The most remarkable aspect of the alien angle as it relates to Noah's Ark came from Don Riggs, whose father worked in the field of photographic analysis for the National Reconnaissance Office in the late 1970s. According to Riggs, just before his death in 1997, his father revealed to him a startling story concerning records and imagery on Noah's Ark that had been referred to the NRO for analysis by a small group of people stationed at Wright-Patterson Air Force Base in Dayton, Ohio, and who were attached to an operation called Project Moon Dust.

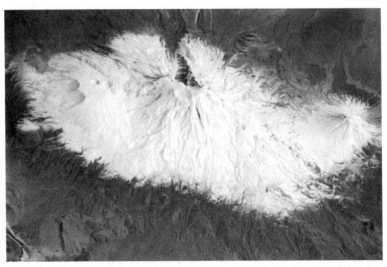

Mt. Ararat: Home to an ancient ark or a crashed UFO? (Copyright NASA.)

If some UFOs are indeed alien spacecraft, and a small percentage of those same craft have crashed to Earth, then among the most important questions currently facing the UFO research community are surely: (a) Who within the official world is responsible for coordinating the retrieval of such craft?; (b) How are those tasked with the recoveries seemingly able to secure UFO crash sites with such apparent speed and ease?; (c) To where is the recovered extraterrestrial material and debris taken?; and (d) Can we identify the key and integral players that have been implicated in this particular controversy?

To try to answer at least some of those particularly important questions, we have to turn our attentions to an official U.S. military intelligence project named Moon Dust that—from the 1950s onward—was housed at Fort Belvoir, Virginia, and whose mandate, according to officially declassified documentation, was to recover and exploit foreign and exotic technologies. Although it is apparent that the bulk of the work of Project Moon Dust was directed toward the careful capture and analysis of crashed Soviet space satellites and rocket debris, there are strong indications that Moon Dust's work may have extended into far stranger—and possibly even extra-terrestrial—realms, too, some of which had a major bearing upon the story of Noah's Ark.

A November 1961 Air Force Intelligence document pertaining to the activities of and guidelines for Moon Dust personnel, specifically at their base of operations within the 1127th Air Activities Group at Fort Belvoir (known in other incarnations as the 4602nd Air Intelligence Service Squadron, and the 1006th Air Intelligence Service Squadron), carefully outlined the nature and the scope of Moon Dust. Titled *AFCIN Intelligence Team Personnel*, the document revealed that with respect to the 1127th Air Activities Group: "In addition to their staff duty assignments, intelligence team personnel have peacetime duty functions in support of such Air Force projects as Moon Dust, Blue Fly, and UFO, and other AFCIN directed quick reaction projects which require intelligence team operational capabilities" (Department of the Air Force, 1961).

The author of the document added: "Unidentified Flying Objects (UFO): Headquarters USAF has established a program for investigation of reliably reported unidentified flying objects within the United States. Blue Fly: Operation Blue Fly has been established to facilitate expeditious delivery to Foreign Technology Division of Moon Dust or other items of great technical interest. Moon Dust: As a specialized aspect of its overall material exploitation program Headquarters USAF has established Project Moon Dust to locate, recover, and deliver descended foreign space vehicles" (Ibid.).

But what of the Noah's Ark connection to Project Moon Dust?

Blowing the Whistle

Don Riggs said that his father told him the file he saw referenced how Moon Dust personnel had begun to take an interest in the Ark story in the late 1960s—intriguingly, around the very same time that David Duckworth was reportedly exposed to Ark data at the Smithsonian Institution. Riggs stated that his father discussed with him his knowledge of seven black-and-white photographs that appeared to show the Ark at very close quarters on the mountain. He further explained that two of the photographs displayed what was, beyond any shadow of a doubt, a "very large, *metallic-looking* [emphasis added] rectangular object sticking partly out of the ice. No way was this wood, he said, like an Ark would be made of," Riggs stated (Redfern, 2007).

Riggs went on to say that the photographs had been immediately classified after they had been taken "at some point around '59 by a U-2 plane [sic]," and had been circulated to various elements of American Intelligence in an effort to try to determine what was buried under the thick ice and snow of Mt. Ararat. "My dad said the pictures on their own didn't really answer much, because of the mountain being so inaccessible, apart from by planes and spy-cameras, satellites. No one was able then to get to the exact right place on-foot to check it out," said Riggs (Ibid.).

Significantly, however, Riggs maintained his father revealed that at some point in the summer of 1975 a covert mission was initiated in which a team of what Riggs describes as "Delta-Force-type guys, I suppose, or something like that," were covertly "dropped" in the area late one night, and who "found their way to the site." Riggs said his father was given access to these latter photographs for analysis some time after the initial, earlier batch was supplied to him (Ibid.).

Riggs added that a lengthy report was filed by the team leader and was duly sent to a group that "my dad said was called the Moon Dust." He added that his father made it clear to him the anomaly was extensively damaged, appeared to be very old, was deeply embedded in the ice, "was vacant inside as if it had been trashed, and was just a shell of metal," and was certainly not "just a big, old, wooden boat" (Ibid.).

Reportedly, Riggs divulged, the documentation had its home at Wright-Patterson, "and a [courier] was told to take it to my dad, who was asked to look at the photographs to see if anything could be seen that would give clues to this thing" (Ibid.). Wright-Patterson, it will have been noted,

was where Robert Livingston was exposed to a photograph
of the Ark in 1954.

"*Everything*," Riggs added with emphasis, "had a Moon
Dust stamp—on each page. There was no history of the Ark
or whatever it was, and nothing that was background information for my dad to work with," apart from the description
of the object and the photos, and brief data on the team that
had landed and taken the pictures. Harold Riggs was never
told by his Wright-Patterson contact what the object was,
only to make an evaluation of the photographs. But, said
Riggs, "there was talk with the guys dad worked with of one
thing that always stands out for me," namely that "this was
not just like a big old boat or Ark. My dad said it looked like
a metal device that had crashed into the ice—probably thousands of years ago, they heard from someone" (Ibid.).

Riggs concluded briefly, but with overwhelming significance: "The talk was of a UFO, really, colliding on the mountain [sic] way back whenever, and causing the Ark story to
begin as we're told it today in the Bible" (Ibid.).

As the previous scenario demonstrates, staff from both
Wright-Patterson and Moon Dust appear to have played a
central role in the saga of Noah's Ark. Moreover, the fact
that the aforementioned Robert Livingston was linked with
Fort Belvoir's Topographic Engineering Center is highly significant: At one point in its history, Project Moon Dust personnel specifically had their base of operations within the
1127th Air Activities Group at the same base—Fort Belvoir.

An E.T. Armada

The theories of George Van Tassel and the revelations
of Don Riggs aside, we see additional evidence of links between people allied to the Noah's Ark saga and the UFO

controversy. Someone who was copied on, and kept appraised of, much of the CIA's documentation on Noah's Ark, even after his official retirement from the world of espionage, was a man named Arthur C. Lundahl, who happened to be a former director of the Agency's National Photographic Interpretation Center. As well as being a player in the Noah's Ark controversy, albeit under presently and admittedly unclear circumstances, Lundahl had a significant link to the world of UFOs and official secrecy, too.

As just one of many examples on record, according to the text of a classified report prepared by Major Robert Friend of the U.S. Air Force's UFO research program Project Blue Book, a secret meeting was held on July 9, 1959, at a CIA office in Washington, D.C., under the direction of Lundahl, at which Lundahl discussed the possibility of trying to contact alien entities by the means of ESP and psychic phenomena. Clearly, then, the man had his finger in a number of pies of the paranormal variety.

Then there is the story of Senator Barry Goldwater, who served as a major general in the Air Force, as the Republican Party's nominee for President of the United States in the 1964 election, and as the chairman of the U.S. government's Senate Intelligence Committee. On September 1, 1978, Goldwater wrote a letter to the then-director of the CIA, Stansfield Turner, that began: "You may think this is a screwball request and it may be, but I would like to know if you can do anything about it" (Goldwater, 1978).

Goldwater went on to ask if "satellite photography" could be searched "to determine whether or not something in the way of an archaeological find might be located near or on top of" Mount Ararat. Goldwater explained to the CIA director that he had received a letter "from a man in whom

I have great confidence, who certainly is no nut, who knows Turkey rather well but who feels that there is reason to believe the Ark may be resting at or near the top of the mount. I assure that I will keep this at any classification you want it kept and if you desire me to go to the devil, I know the way." The CIA responded that it had no data on file suggesting the Ark had been identified or located anywhere on Mt. Ararat, or indeed anywhere else (Ibid.).

Goldwater's comment that he would understand if the Ark issue was of "any classification" that might result in the CIA telling him to "go to the devil" is extremely reminiscent of a very weird situation in which Goldwater found himself more than a decade earlier (Ibid.).

On March 28, 1975, Goldwater wrote the following highly thought-provoking words to a UFO researcher named Shlomo Arnon: "The subject of UFOs is one that has interested me for some long time. About ten or twelve years ago I made an effort to find out what was in the building at Wright-Patterson Air Force Base where the information is stored that has been collected by the Air Force, and I was understandably denied this request. It is still classified above Top Secret" (Goldwater, 1975).

Goldwater later clarified and expanded on this by revealing that U.S. Air Force General Curtis Le May had given Goldwater absolute holy hell for daring to ask if he could see the USAF's top-secret UFO data rumored to be stored at Wright-Patterson—which possibly included preserved alien corpses and recovered extra-terrestrial hardware and technology. Moreover, Le May told Goldwater, in just about the sternest of all tones conceivably possible, not to even *think* about bringing up this matter with him again—*ever*.

If Goldwater, who had a deep, personal interest in UFOs, had even the slightest inklings or suspicions that Noah's Ark was somehow linked to matters of an alien nature, rather than to anything of a specifically religious nature, then this might very possibly explain why he anticipated being told to go to hell by the CIA in 1978, in much the same way that Le May had less than tactfully suggested to him years earlier in relation to rumors of captured UFOs held at Wright-Patterson Air Force Base.

But, if the story of Noah's Ark, and the varied additional worldwide tales of huge vessels constructed in times past to survive a looming cataclysmic flood, *is* somehow connected to the UFO puzzle, then what might lie at the heart of that controversial connection? An answer, maybe, comes from researcher Bruce Rux, who believes the origins of many biblical accounts, legends, and stories can be traced back to the actions and presence of ancient extra-terrestrial visitors to our planet. Rux makes a very good point: "The Gilgamesh Epic does not say that Noah took two of every animal on board the ship with him, but rather 'the seeds of life,' which makes considerably more sense if a highly technical DNA preservation scenario is allowed" (Rux, 1996).

Is this what was really at the heart of the legend of Noah's Ark, and the many other worldwide stories of massive ships reportedly built millennia ago to survive a terrifying, planet-wide devastation? Namely, that highly advanced aliens, keenly aware of an all-encompassing, irreversible catastrophe looming on the horizon, fashioned fantastic and gigantic craft, aboard which life, both human and animal—but possibly wholly in the form of DNA, rather than as cumbersome walking, talking, flying or growling specimens—could be saved and preserved when the terrifying flood waters began to disastrously rise? Rather than being boats of a very earthly nature, were the Arks really spacecraft from faraway worlds? Was an alien armada engaged in some sort of salvage mission to ensure terrestrial life continued after the flood? George Van Tassel certainly thought so, and the FBI most definitely sat up and took notice when he said precisely that, as did the CIA and the National Security Agency, both of which held copies of the FBI's files on Van Tassel. Perhaps, after studying the Ark issue to a deep degree, Project Moon Dust personnel, whose work was *heavily* UFO-connected, concluded likewise.

And that, so far as is known outside of secret, governmental, inner sanctums, is where the story of the U.S. government's curious interest in Noah's Ark ends. But, there were plenty of other things of an ancient, historic, and religious nature that kept officialdom busy behind the scenes for years.

LEVITATION AND
THE PHARAOHS

The controversy-filled theory that a number of human-kind's most impressive and legendary constructions, such as the pyramids of Egypt, the similar structures that pepper whole swathes of South and Central America, and England's Stonehenge, were built via the use of fantastic technologies long lost to the fog of time, is one that provokes a great deal of interest and attention, as well as loud and vexed voices.

In essence, the amazing theory suggests that the raising and placing of massive stone blocks in eras long past was achieved by the manipulation and nullification of gravitational forces or anti-gravity, in simple terms. Or via the use of groundbreaking acoustic-levitation, technology that allows for the suspension of and manipulation of matter in the air via the use of carefully directed sound waves. Marie D. Jones and Larry Flaxman describe acoustic-levitation as a means to introduce "two opposing sound frequencies with interfering sound waves, thus creating a resonant zone that allows the levitation to occur. Theoretically, to move a levitating object, simply change or alter the two sound waves and tweak accordingly" (Jones and Flaxman, 2009).

Even more sensationally, the U.S. military has taken a keen and provable interest in these particular matters and beliefs. The story continues that the Pentagon has secretly taken much of its inspiration in investigating these undeniably alternative issues from studying the work of authors in the field of ancient astronaut research. But, before we can even begin to probe such controversy-filled waters, a body of background data of the historical variety is most certainly required.

Egyptian Enigmas

Beyond any shadow of doubt, of the many and varied architectural achievements of the human race, the pyramids of Egypt must surely top the list in terms of provoking deep awe and amazement—and a great deal of unbridled controversy and debate, too. Conventional Egyptology suggests that the pyramids were built during what are today termed the Old and Middle Kingdoms of Egypt. That's to say from around the third millennium BC to roughly 1650 BC. The reason for their construction: almost certainly to act as tombs for the pharaohs, so convention tells us.

Levitation: the secret of the pyramids?
(Copyright Felix Bonfils, 1878)

By far the most famous of all the many and varied Egyptian pyramids are those that comprise the Giza Necropolis, located around 15 miles outside of the old city of Cairo. And although the Necropolis is viewed as being very much a unified entity, it is the Great Pyramid of Giza that attracts so much attention. Hardly surprising: The huge structure practically commands respect from all those who flock to view its massive, immovable form. While discussion continues with regard to why the Great Pyramid was built, most scholars take the view that it was created to serve as a tomb for the pharaoh Khufu, who reigned during the fourth dynasty—a period that extended from 2613 BC to 2494 BC. And its dimensions and statistical data almost boggle the mind.

The Great Pyramid is in excess of 450 feet in height, has four sides that, before a degree of erosion set in, were originally more than 750 feet long, was constructed with more than half a million tons of mortar, and has an overall mass of almost 6 million tons. That's right: *6 million*. And here's where things get decidedly interesting. Most Egyptian scholars take the view that the Great Pyramid was constructed over a period of approximately two decades. But, given the sheer number of limestone blocks that comprise the huge form—2.3 million, some of which weigh between a staggering 25 and 80 tons—this would have required truly incredible workmanship to complete such a task in that particular time frame. Mainstream archaeology assures us that such monumental workmanship was achieved via the use of nothing stranger than sheer human willpower and brute force. But whether that same willpower and brute-force were provided by volunteers, slaves, or a combination of both is a matter of ongoing debate.

As for the actual methods of construction, the prevailing view is that the great stones were cut from quarries using copper chisels, at least one of which, at Aswan, was located in excess of 500 miles from the Giza Necropolis. Then, by methods possibly involving a complex combination of ropes, ramps, and levers, the huge, multi-ton blocks were dragged, rolled, hauled, pulled, and pushed into place. Such a scenario sounds as amazing as it does doubtful and dubious. But, there is another potential explanation for how the pyramids of Egypt—along with numerous other ancient complexes and creations—were crafted. And it, too, is undeniably amazing, but for very different, and wildly alternative, reasons.

A Book of Secrets

Abu al-Hasan Ali al-Mas'udi, otherwise known as the Herodotus of the Arabs, was a prolific 10th-century writer born in Baghdad in 896 AD who faithfully and carefully prepared an immense, 30-volume series of texts that told the history of the world, based upon his personal, extensive travels to lands far, wide, and exotic. His impressive and dedicated treks took him to such varied parts of the globe as India, East Africa, Egypt, Syria, and Armenia. He was also a skilled seaman who traversed the Mediterranean, the Caspian Sea, the Red Sea, and the Indian Ocean. And it was during his many excursions to such places that al-Mas'udi collected the equally many tales, stories, and legends that made their way into that aforementioned and priceless multi-volume work. Its collective title, translated into English, was *The Meadows of Gold and Mines of Gems*. But, for all of the fascinating data that al-Mas'udi amassed during the course of his numerous wanderings, one piece stands out as being particularly illuminating and highly relevant to the strange story that this chapter tells, too.

Within the pages of his writings, which were completed in 947 AD—nine years before his death at the age of 60—al-Mas'udi noted that in very early Arabic legends there existed an intriguing story suggesting that the creation of the pyramids of Egypt had absolutely nothing to do with the conventional technologies of the era. Rather, al-Mas'udi recorded, tantalizing, centuries-old lore that had come his way during his explorations strongly suggested the pyramids were created by what today we would most likely refer to as some form of levitation.

The incredible story that al-Mas'udi uncovered went like this: When building the pyramids, their creators carefully positioned what was described as magical papyrus underneath the edges of the mighty stones that were to be used in the construction process. Then, one by one, the stones were struck by what was curiously, and rather enigmatically, described only as a rod of metal. Lo and behold, the stones then slowly began to rise into the air, and like dutiful soldiers unquestioningly following orders, proceeded in slow, methodical, single-file fashion a number of feet above a paved pathway surrounded on both sides by similar, mysterious metal rods. For around 150 feet, al-Mas'udi noted, the gigantic stones moved forward, usually with nothing more than the very gentlest of prods from the keeper of the mysterious rod to ensure they stayed on track, before finally, and very softly, settling back to the ground.

At that point, the process was duly repeated. The stones were struck once more, rose up from the surface, and again traveled in the desired direction, for yet another 150 feet or so. And so the strange, repetitive task continued, time and time again, until all of the stones finally reached their ultimate destination. Then, in a distinctly far more complex feat, the stones were struck again, but this time in a fashion that caused them to float even higher into the air. Then, when they reached the desired point, they were carefully, and with incredible ease, manipulated into place, one-by-one, by hand and nothing else, until the huge pyramid in question was finally completed.

Such a scenario sounds manifestly astonishing. Certainly, many might laugh at such amazing assertions. Others might dismiss the whole thing as the ravings of a madman, or the stuff of nothing more than distorted legend and fanciful folklore. The writings of Abu al-Hasan Ali al-Mas'udi, how-ever, do not stand alone. Very similar accounts from centuries long-gone, and from lands as diverse as they are separated by thousands of miles, absolutely abound.

Uplifting Tales

Anomalies researcher Richard E. Mooney noted a story that sounds astonishingly like that of Abu al-Hasan Ali al-Mas'udi, but from the other side of the world: "There is a tradition that appears in the mythology of the Americas that the priests 'made the stones light,' so that they were moved easily." He adds that "this connects with the legend of levitation, which may have referred originally to an actual technique or device, long since forgotten" (Mooney, 1974).

In addition, researcher John Anthony West, who has deeply studied the role sound played in the life of the ancient Egyptians, highlighted two issues of importance and relevance: (a) today, our admittedly very tentative acoustic-based technology research has achieved a degree of lift in small objects by maintaining them in pockets provoked by the reflection of sound-waves between amplifying disks; and (b) numerous ancient Egyptian structures were built to be deliberately harmonic in nature. That is to say, they show clear evidence of resonation on an audible frequency—a musical note—when struck.

On a similar matter, investigator Andrew Collins noted of Egypt's Great Pyramid: "Precision geometry incorporating harmonics, proportions, and sound acoustics was incorporated into its exterior and interior design." He added: "It has long been known that many of the temples and monuments of Pharaonic Egypt incorporate an intimate knowledge of sound acoustics." Interestingly, Collins said he found evidence to show that within Tibet, right up until the 20th century, certain monastic places held the secrets of "a sonic technology that included the creation of weightlessness in stone blocks" (Collins, 1998).

There's also a highly important third factor, too. Historian Helen Adeline Guerber recorded that the god Apollo "went to assist Neptune...to build the walls of Troy. Scorning to perform any menial tasks, the God of Music seated himself nearby and played such inspiring tunes that the stones moved into place of their own accord" (Guerber, 1893).

On a related matter, the great walls of the Greek city of Thebes have an uncannily similar tale attached to their construction. The walls were said to have been built to the sound of a lyre (a stringed musical instrument) possessed by one Amphion, who, legend tells us, was the son of Zeus, ruler of the Olympians, and Antiope, the daughter of a Greek river god, Asopus. Similarly, the folklore of Phonecia has a tradition of the god Uranus possessing the ability to move huge stones via means near-magical. And, near-identical tales proliferate in relation to the creation of one of the worlds' most famous of all stone wonders: England's Stonehenge. Moreover, Stonehenge is a site that has also attracted the deep attention of military agencies. The full story of that particular enigma is told in a later chapter.

Having now addressed the matter of what the ancients thought about the construction of the pyramids of Egypt and other ancient structures by means they perceived as being near-magical, let us now turn our attentions toward those latter-day, 20th-century students of such controversial matters, their ground-breaking work, and the way in which officialdom carefully and clandestinely monitored their findings and theories.

PYRAMID POWER

Mayan Marvels

When it comes to the issue of the U.S. government's interest in levitation, anti-gravity, the possibility that such extraordinary technology might have been in the hands of the human race thousands of years ago, and even the possibility that this same technology had origins of an extra-terrestrial nature, we have to first turn our attentions to a man named Morris Ketchum Jessup. His is a story of astounding mysteries, long-gone civilizations, government conspiracy, outlandish and alternative experimentation, and, finally, a tragic and deeply controversial death.

Born in 1900, in the town of Rockville, Indiana, Jessup served with the U.S. Army during the latter years of World War I, and had a fascination with both astronomy and mathematics. He secured a bachelor of science from the University of Michigan in 1925, obtained a master of science in the following year, and, had he not elected to radically shake up his life when his academic studies were at their height, would almost certainly have achieved his original goal of being able to officially claim a doctorate in astrophysics. But Jessup had other interests—highly alternative interests—that extended far beyond astronomy and mathematics. They extended right back to the dawn of recorded history, and quite possibly even further back than that.

As someone who had a lifelong fascination with archaeology, Jessup, in the early 1950s, spent several months enthusiastically traveling around Mexico, South America, and much of Central America, including Guatemala and Belize, in search of ancient cities, old ruined lands, and priceless artifacts. Jessup's goal was to secure as deep an understanding as humanly possible of the foundations and cultures of both the Mayans and the Incas.

As for the former, their beginnings can be traced back approximately 4,000 years, and their presence left profound imprints in the Mexican states of Tabasco and Chiapas, as well as much of the Yucatan Peninsula, Honduras, Belize, and Guatemala. The Mayans were a mighty people with an undeniable flair for creating incredible architecture of extraordinary proportions, including sprawling and exotic cities and lavish temples. They were also deeply fascinated by the heavens, astronomy, and mathematics—just like Jessup. This, perhaps, may go some way toward explaining why he so quickly felt such close kinship toward this ancient culture and its activities.

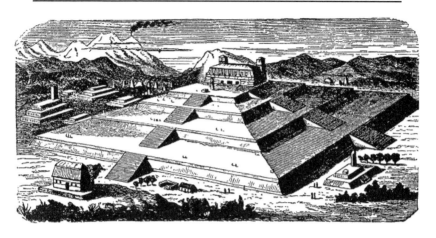

The Great Pyramid of Cholula: an obsession of Morris K. Jessup. (Copyright Nordisk familjebok, 1876.)

Without doubt the greatest, lasting legacies of the Mayans are their very own legendary pyramids that, although certainly somewhat different in design, easily rival those of ancient Egypt in terms of being prime examples of amazing engineering expertise. As evidence of those same extraordinary skills, the Mayan Great Pyramid, which is located at the city of Cholula, in the Mexican state of Puebla, and built in honor of the Mesoamerican god Quetzalcoatl, stands almost 200 feet high, while its base runs to an astonishing 1,300 feet on each of its four sides. But, the Mayan civilization is one that is also steeped in deep mystery. Despite their centuries-long position on the world stage as a major culture, the Mayans were all but gone before the 10th century AD. As for the reason, there is no real clear consensus. Theories include long-lasting droughts, a disastrous outbreak of disease, environmental factors, over-population and an inability to adequately sustain the people, and drastic changes in the climate. Maybe all of those factors played a role in bringing down the Mayans. But, whatever the precise reason for the demise of the Mayans, their incredible stone creations still remain. And, just like their creators, they still generate a great deal of commentary and debate.

Also on the matter of controversy as it relates to the Mayans, it's worth noting an important event that occurred in 2010. In Cancun, in November of that year, the *Pan-American/Iberian Meeting on Acoustics* was held. The event covered a great deal of new revelations in the field of the physics of sound. But one particular presentation stood out. It was that of David Lubman who, in 1998, had a paper published in the *Journal of the Acoustical Society of America* that demonstrated the extraordinary acoustics in evidence in certain structures constructed by the Mayans. Lubman discussed how clapping one's hands in front of the El Castillo pyramid in Mexico's Yucatan creates a sound astonishingly like the song of a quetzal bird. This was echoed by Nico Declercq of Ghent University, Belgium, who uncovered yet another strange acoustic effect: People sitting at the base of the pyramid reported that the footsteps of visitors to the site who were walking around at higher levels sounded remarkably like rainfall. Lubman said: "I think the pyramids were essentially echo machines, built to inspire spiritual feelings" (Vergano, 2010).

Of course, the previous information is not intended to bolster the idea that the Mayans used acoustic technology in the creation of their fantastic structures. It does, however, further demonstrate that as with the Egyptians, and also in relation to the legends concerning the creation of the Turkish city of Troy and, as we will see later with Stonehenge, England, tales of extraordinary acoustics and amazing, ancient stone complexes go together hand-in-glove. But there is one story that *does* accord well with the notion that some form of levitation may have played a role in the construction of certain Mayan structures.

Uxmal is, today at least, an overwhelmingly ruined city of the Mayans, the remains of which are found in the Yucatan Peninsula. Mayan chronicles say that the initial foundations of Uxmal were laid about 500 AD, with the peak of its construction occurring in the 800s and 900s, after which the city went into a slow but steady decline and was largely abandoned by the 1500s. Far more interesting than the history of Uxmal, however, is the lasting legend that it was built by a mysterious dwarf-like entity, or entities, that had the eerie ability to command huge stones into the air merely by whistling at them. Or by utilizing some curious form of amazing, acoustic-driven technology, we might by now be inclined to argue.

The Incredible Incas

Regarding the Incas, they flourished in the Peruvian highlands in the early 1200s and, by the 1500s, could boast of being nothing less than a definitive empire, having come to hold sway over whole swathes of the western parts of South America, including significant portions of, among others, Chile, Argentina, and Bolivia. That is, at least, until 1526 when Spanish conquistadores led by Francisco Pizarro descended upon their civilization, and the face of Incan society quickly and dramatically changed for the worst. Overwhelmed by both the conquering Spaniards and devastating outbreaks of smallpox, typhus, diphtheria, and measles, the Incan empire was a broken and spent one by the early 1600s. But, just like the Mayans, the Incas left behind an incredible and vast body of architecture that also attracted the sharp mind and eagle eyes of Morris K. Jessup.

One of the places that so fascinated Jessup was Tiwan-aku, a precursor to the Incan society, the remnants of which are situated near the shore of Lake Titicaca in Western Bolivia, an area dominated by regular volcanic activity. Notably, local Indian legend told of the city's very first inhabitants possessing archaic secrets that allowed them to raise huge stones into the air by the mere sound of a trumpet. A pattern, we see, is clearly developing: It extended from Greece to Egypt and from the Yucatan to Stonehenge, and it involved the raising of massive stone blocks by some form of technology that appeared to nullify gravity, or in which acoustic technology played some form of role. Or both.

Eclipsing just about all of the major achievements of the Incas is a large historic complex called Machu Picchu, which sits almost 8,000 feet above sea level, on mountainous terrain in Peru's picturesque Urubamba Valley. Machu Picchu—the construction of which is generally accepted as having started during the 1400s, and is noted for a trio of particularly impressive structures, the Temple of the Sun, the Room of the Three Windows, and the Intihuatana—is viewed by many scholars and researchers as having been a place of deep religious significance and worship.

Machu Picchu: a Peruvian puzzle.
(Copyright Bingham 1911.)

Not only that, Machu Picchu is also renowned for its astronomical relevance. The Intihuatana, for example, which is actually a large stone pillar whose title broadly translates to "for tying the Sun," has been intrinsically linked with the coming of the winter solstice and Incan fears that, as the nights got progressively darker and longer, so our Sun would one day fully disappear, possibly never to return and illuminate our world. The result: The worried people of Machu Picchu performed complex and dedicated ceremonies at the Intihuatana to ensure the survival of the Sun throughout the period of the solstice. More intriguingly, Machu Picchu is home to an astronomical observatory where, through its northeast-facing window, the viewer can secure an excellent view of the rising of the Pleiades, or the Seven Sisters, a cluster of stars located in the constellation of Taurus.

And, it was this astronomical link to Machu Picchu that so fascinated Morris K. Jessup, to whom we now return.

The Case for the UFO

Deeply relevant to the story of Morris K. Jessup is the time frame in which his expeditions south of the border took place: the early 1950s. Although Jessup had visited both the Yucatan and Peru as early as the 1920s, had studied the sources of crude rubber in the Amazon for the U.S. Department of Agriculture, and spent time in the jungles of Central America with funding supplied by the Carnegie Institute, it was four little-known and seldom-discussed trips that Jessup made in late 1952—one to Peru, a second to Mexico, a third to Bolivia, and a final one to Belize—that led him on a path that crossed directly with that of the UFO controversy, which was at its height at that time. It can be reasonably argued that, for Jessup, those paths didn't just cross—they converged in spectacular style.

In July 1952, only mere months before Jessup set off on his trek into the mysterious past, veritable shockwaves rumbled and reverberated throughout the U.S. government, military, and Intelligence communities when, during the course of two weekends, multiple UFO encounters were reported throughout the nation's capital of Washington, D.C.—many by Air Force pilots and ground-based radar personnel. It was this wave of encounters that led the Air Force to quietly advise J. Edgar Hoover's FBI that they could not rule out the possibility that at least some UFOs were the products of visiting martians.

Having an interest in matters of an outer space nature already, Jessup took careful note of the UFO puzzle from its beginnings in 1947—and particularly the huge wave of encounters of July 1952—and followed the debate over the nature of the phenomenon with ever-growing enthusiasm. And it was after having visited South America, Central America, and Mexico in the early 1950s, where he further studied the fantastic structures of the Mayans, the Incas, and a plethora of ancient Mexican cultures, that Jessup came to a notable conclusion. The awe-inspiring structures of all these long-gone civilizations, Jessup believed, simply could not have come to fruition without the benefit of outside help, the denizens of other words themselves: extra-terrestrials.

Jessup noted in 1955 something that practically harked back to the ancient days of Abu al-Hasan Ali al-Mas'udi himself: "I have seen and touched stonework carved out of the solid mountains of rock in South America, which certainly antedate the Andean glaciers, and almost as certainly predate the formation of the mountain themselves. This work is superior in technique to that accomplished by our currently mechanized civilization. Much of that construction, sculpture and tunneling could only have been accomplished by 'forces' different from those in use by us today. The quandary is largely resolvable by admitting to a levitating force... The lifting of the ancient megalithic structures too, must have surely come through levitation" (Jessup, 1955).

Among those very same ancient megalithic structures that Jessup concluded were built via the utilization of levitation were the enigmatic figures of Easter Island and the great Stone of the Pregnant Woman that sits at Baalbek in Lebanon's Bekaa Valley, which weighs in at a near-unbelievable *1,000 tons*. And, it's fair to say, Jessup practically sneered and scoffed at the very idea that these creations were the work of nothing but countless people equipped with not much more than rollers, ramps, ropes, and pulleys.

Jessup conceded, however, that though such technology was a reality, its availability, scope, and usage seemed to have been sorely limited to certain key areas of the planet. Those areas were the Middle East, India, Pakistan, China and its immediate surroundings, select parts of Europe, and much of South America, Mexico, and Central America. But, Australia, Africa, Canada, the United States, and the vast expanses of Russia seemed not—in Jessup's eyes, anyway—to have played an overwhelmingly large role in the development of levitation-themed technology in the past.

Also on his travels, Jessup uncovered information relative to certain well-preserved, ancient Oriental records on levitation. They were said to have been guarded with near-paranoid zeal in a number of well-hidden monasteries in various parts of the Himalayas and central China. More significantly, Jessup made the observation that, in precisely the same way the U.S. government wished to get its hands on the technological marvels of the ancients, the secrets of levitation held in the Himalayas had prompted Soviet authorities to try to find, and then plunder the stone-raising marvels of, these same elusive monasteries.

As his research into the puzzles of the past escalated, Jessup came to believe that perhaps more than 100,000 years ago there existed on the Earth a mighty, technologically advanced civilization that ultimately came to a catastrophic destruction, and a very quick and unforeseen destruction, too. Jessup—as his personal letters to colleagues strongly indicate—seemed obsessed by the idea that the levitation technology, and the powerful overlords behind its creation, vanished with great and sudden violence in a long-distant era.

Perhaps, Jessup considered, the end came as a result of massive military conflict. Or, maybe, overwhelming destruction was the result of a natural disaster, such as a worldwide deluge that overtook the planet and led to the creation of countless flood myths and legends of the very type discussed in previous chapters of this book. But of one thing Jessup was fully certain: This ancient race was responsible for laying down the foundations of the legends of Atlantis, and the cultures that he believed finally rose long after its collapse, including those of Central America, South America, India, Egypt, and Tibet. Or in Jessup's very own terminology: the reviving remnants.

But how, precisely, did Jessup believe such astounding levitation was achieved? He certainly had a few ideas: "I have used the word 'levitation' as a substitute for power or force. I have suggested that flying saucers used some means of reacting with the gravitational field. In this way they could apply accelerations or lifting forces to all particles of a body, inside and outside, simultaneously, and not through external force applied by pressure, or harness, to the surface only. I believe that this same, or a similar force was used to move stones in very ancient times" (Jessup, 1957).

All of this could, quite rightly, be seen as nothing more than the highly alternative theories of one man who had deeply studied the mysteries of the past, and who then came to a series of remarkable and undeniably alternative conclusions in the process. But Jessup's ideas, and his book discussing such issues, *The Case for the UFO*, led to something sensational that Jessup almost certainly never anticipated. Combined, they prompted the careful and concerned attention of a certain significant office within the heart of the U.S. Navy.

CONSPIRACIES OF THE NAVAL KIND

Not long after the publication of *The Case for the UFO*, Morris K. Jessup became the recipient of a series of extremely strange letters from a certain Carlos Allende (aka Carl Allen) of Pennsylvania. In his controversial correspondence, Allende commented on Jessup's theories relative to levitation among the ancients, and also gave details of an alleged secret experiment conducted by the U.S. Navy in the Philadelphia Naval Yard in October 1943. According to Allende's incredible tale, during the experiment, a warship was rendered optically invisible and teleported to and back from Norfolk, Virginia, in a few minutes, the incredible feat supposedly having supposedly been accomplished by applying Albert Einstein's never-completed unified field theory.

85

Allende elaborated that the ship used in the experiment was the *DE 173 USS Eldridge*; and, moreover, that he, Allende, had actually witnessed one of the attempts to render both the ship and its crew invisible from his position out at sea on-board a steamer called the *SS Andrew Furuseth*. From the safety of the *Furuseth*, Allende said he looked on with amazement as the air all around the ship first turned slightly dark, before taking on the appearance of a green fog. Then, even more amazingly, the *Eldridge* suddenly vanished from sight—literally.

If Allende was telling the truth, the Navy, as well as grasping invisibility, had also tapped into the secret of teleportation of the type demonstrated in fictional, on-screen format in *Star Trek* and *The Fly*. On these very matters, Allende made the disturbing claim that not only did the experiment render many of the crew members insane, but some, he said, even literally vanished from the ship while the test was at its height, never to be seen again. Others reportedly became fused into the metal hull of the ship itself, destined to die horrific and agonizing deaths. Jessup was both excited and not a little disturbed by what Allende related to him during the course of a number of communications in 1956. But even Jessup, for all the high-strangeness that had by now enveloped him, thanks to Allende, was scarcely prepared for the next chapter in this strange story.

The Navy Takes Note of Jessup

In 1956, a copy of Jessup's *The Case for the UFO* was mailed anonymously to the U.S. Navy's Office of Naval Research (ONR) in Washington, D.C, and was turned over to Major Darrell L. Ritter. But this was no run-of-the-mill edition of Jessup's controversial tome. The pages of the

book in question were interspersed with handwritten comments—albeit in several different colors of ink, no less,
and in a weird combination of both uppercase and lowercase letters—which suggested an extensive knowledge of
UFOs, their means of motion, and the culture and ethos
of the beings occupying these same UFOs, all described in
undeniably pseudo-scientific terms. Those same comments
and scrawls, to the uninitiated at least, read like the work of
a madman, or several madmen, given that the annotations
were allegedly provided by three mysteriously-titled people:
Jemi, Mr. A., and Mr. B.

Two officers who were then assigned to the ONR,
Captain Sidney Sherby and Commander George W. Hoover,
the latter being the Special Projects Officer with the ONR
at the time, exhibited particular interest in Jessup's *The Case
for the UFO* and its attendant annotations. The pair wasted
no time at all in tracking Jessup down via his publisher. And,
having done so, Sherby and Hoover did something else
manifestly unusual: They quickly invited Jessup, come to
Washington, D.C., to discuss both his book and the curious
handwritten notes included in the copy in the Navy's possession. Jessup, by now even more worried, but also excited
about what was afoot, gave the invitation some thought,
and, probably inevitably, agreed to fly to D.C. for a face-to-
face meeting.

On arrival in D.C. Jessup was taken out for dinner (almost certainly to ensure he was placed in a relaxed state of
mind), and was then provided with a pleasant hotel room
that night and, the next morning, a hearty breakfast. Then,
hours later, in an office of the ONR, vigorous questioning
about Jessup's book, the theories and data contained therein, and, of course, the discussion of the vanishing ship and

the strange annotations of Jemi, Mr. A., and Mr. B. began in earnest fashion. When Sherby and Hoover presented Jessup with the copy of the book that had been anonymously mailed to the ONR, it took Jessup barely an instant to realize that the curious handwriting that filled its pages matched that of Carlos Allende. He told the officers precisely that, and openly shared with them the contents of the curious letters he had received from Allende.

The Philideplphia Naval Yard: A hotbed of secrets. (Copyright U.S. Navy.)

Despite the astounding nature of Allende's claims, the Navy then did something even more amazing: It secretly arranged and paid for copies of Jessup's book to be made by the Varo Corporation of Garland, Texas. This was an incredibly tedious task for Miss Michael Ann Dunn, who was the secretary to the president of Varo. She had the highly unenviable task of having to first retype Jessup's entire 200-plus-page book in its entirety, and carefully add—in their original colors, style, and odd combination of capitalized and lowercase lettering—all of Allende's annotations, exactly as they appeared in the original edition as mailed to Major Darrell L. Ritter. Then, Dunn had to run off no less than 25 copies of this new edition of Jessup's book, one of which was apparently provided to Jessup, but which later vanished from his office. Unlike the *USS Eldridge*, however, Jessup's copy of the Varo edition did not put in a re-appearance. Rather mysteriously, the Navy will only say today of this particular aspect of the perplexing affair that (a) both Sherby and Hoover left the Navy years ago, (b) they took all of their personal items with them, and (c) the ONR no longer possesses even a single copy of the two dozen or so copies of Jessup's annotated book. Or, rather: Don't ask questions that don't concern you.

It's worth noting that although the Navy, today, admits that the ONR did indeed take note of Jessup's *The Case for the UFO*, and that he did visit its offices to discuss the contents of the book, it insists that the interest shown in Jessup and his work was wholly personal on the part of Sherby and Hoover. In other words—officially speaking, anyway—it was actually nothing to do with the Navy at all, and whatever its employees wished to do in their free time was entirely their own business and not that of the U.S. Navy.

That particular claim, however, is thrown into major doubt by the revelation that the Navy officially picked up the entire tab for Jessup's flight, as well as all his hotel, taxi, and meal expenses incurred during his time spent in D.C.

Moreover, Anne Lykins Genzlinger, who deeply studied the Jessup affair in the late-1970s and early-1980s, noted that Sherby and Hoover were attached to a naval program designed to place a satellite in near-Earth orbit and may have "also been involved in gravity research." This, commented Genzlinger, was very possibly the reason why the ONR pair showed such "unusual interest" in Jessup's book. All of these particular revelations do not accord at all well with the idea that the interest in Jessup's book was simply off-the-record. They collectively suggest the precise opposite (Genzlinger, 1981).

A Controversial Death

Levitation in the distant past, floating stones, pyramids built by anti-gravity, strange and horrific deaths at sea, a vanishing ship, and the notable attention of the Office of Naval Research: Jessup not surprisingly left Washington, D.C. with his head spinning and wondering what he had gotten himself into. It was not an issue he was destined to muse upon for a long time, however. Jessup was found dead in his car on April 29, 1959, at the Dale County Park in Florida. Officially, the cause was suicide as a result of carbon-monoxide poisoning. Proponents of this theory note that, in 1958, Jessup's wife, Rubye, walked out on him, and he was certainly showing signs of depression as a result of this unfortunate turmoil in his private life. That Jessup's books were no longer attracting much of an audience, and that a number of his future book projects and ideas received nothing but letters of rejection from his publishers, were also considered potential factors that may have led to despondency and death by Jessup's very own hand.

But there is another issue that just cries out to be explored: Jessup's end came just 24 hours after he contacted a close friend and colleague who shared his passion for ancient civilizations and the mysteries of the past—Dr. Manson Valentine—and asked for a meeting the very next day. The reason was to discuss with Valentine an exciting new breakthrough Jessup claimed to have made in relation to the notorious story of the vanishing warship at the Philadelphia Naval Yard in 1943. It was a breakthrough that Jessup felt highly uncomfortable discussing on the telephone, so a face-to-face discussion was arranged. Sadly, and perhaps even sinisterly, it never came to pass. Whether as a result of his own tragic actions, or the far darker and colder hands of a hired assassin, Jessup never got to share that new breakthrough with Valentine. To this day, however, rumors continue to circulate among those who believe in the USS Eldridge's disappearing act that Jessup's death may have been a prime example of nothing less than a state-sponsored murder, specifically undertaken as part of an official effort to hide the truth about the strange story of the invisible ship and Jessup's research into ancient levitation. Unsurprisingly, the Navy has been very careful not to comment upon the controversy surrounding Jessup's untimely demise. But it does have an opinion with regard to what it believes may really have led to the legend of the experiment at the Philadelphia Naval Yard:

"Personnel at the Fourth Naval District believe that the questions surrounding the so-called 'Philadelphia Experiment' arise from quite routine research which occurred during World War II at the Philadelphia Naval Shipyard. Until recently, it was believed that the foundation for the apocryphal stories arose from degaussing experiments which have the effect of making a ship undetectable or 'invisible' to magnetic mines" (Department of the Navy, 1996).

The Navy elaborates: "Degaussing is a process in which a system of electrical cables are [sic] installed around the circumference of a ship's hull, running from bow to stern on both sides. A measured electrical current is passed through these cables to cancel out the ship's magnetic field. Degaussing equipment was installed in the hull of Navy ships and could be turned on whenever the ship was in waters that might contain magnetic mines, usually shallow waters in combat areas. It could be said that degaussing, correctly done, makes a ship 'invisible' to the sensors of magnetic mines, but the ship remains visible to the human eye, radar, and underwater listening devices" (Department of the Navy, 2000).

Just to confuse things even further, however, the Navy has also offered a further theory to explain the effects on the crew: "Another likely genesis of the bizarre stories about levitation, teleportation and effects on human crewmembers might be attributed to experiments with the generating plant of a destroyer, the *USS Timmerman*. In the 1950's this ship was part of an experiment to test the effects of a small, high frequency generator providing 1000 hz, instead of the standard 400hz. The higher frequency generator produced corona discharges, and other well-known phenomena associated with high frequency generators. None of the crew suffered effects from the experiment" (Department of the Navy, 1996).

Allende and Anti-Gravity

Finally, there is one issue of paramount importance, and certainly of deep relevance to this book, that many investigators of the Jessup affair have overlooked, misinterpreted, or just outright ignored. That Carlos Allende focused much of the content of his letters to Jessup on the alleged invisibility-driven events in wartime Philadelphia is something that has led commentators to suggest this was specifically the reason why the Navy took such careful notice of the curiously annotated version of *The Case for the UFO* that reached the ONR.

But what has been seldom highlighted is that, in complete contrast to the letters sent to Jessup, most of the notes scrawled in the pages of the copy of Jessup's book that the Navy received anonymously had *nothing* at all to do with whatever did or did not occur in the waters off Philadelphia in 1943. Rather, Allende's annotations to *The Case for the UFO* had *everything* to do with Jessup's writings on how and why he believed ancient civilizations used levitation to construct the pyramids of Egypt, Central America, and South America. So, there can be no doubt on this particular issue, in one specific part of *The Case for the UFO*, where he commented on the levitation theories, Jessup wrote that, in his opinion, the blocks utilized in the construction of ancient megaliths were simply too huge and unwieldy to be moved by any means beyond levitation. In the copy of the book in the Navy's hands, Jessup's words on this matter had been carefully, and thickly, underlined by Allende.

Allende continued to laboriously underline additional, relevant sentences on this same issue in precisely the same fashion. Those underlined sections included data on "gravity nullification," a very ancient "mechanized civilization," "levitating forces," "gravity control," "the secrets of ancient flight," "massive unfinished stones" (including the 1,000-ton monster at Baalbek), "levitator"-technology developed by the Peruvians in times past, the manipulation of "gravitational fields," and, maybe most notable of all, repeated references to a deeply enigmatic, and long-gone race of people who possessed now-poorly understood technologies that allowed them to maneuver huge stones on a scale and via methods wholly unparalleled even today (Jessup, 1955).

As this demonstrates, a very strong case can be made that, although the U.S. Navy most certainly did not ignore Allende's controversial claims on the story of the vanishing ship in his letters sent to Jessup, it took far greater interest in the portions of Jessup's book dealing with levitation-based technology used by a world that existed long before ours was even the very tiniest glimmer. After all, does flying Jessup into Washington, D.C., providing him with a hotel room, and even paying to have printed more than two dozen copies of his book sound like a lack of interest, or something that merely attracted the attention of a couple of ONR employees in their free, after-work hours? No, it most assuredly does not.

Morris K. Jessup's research into the mysteries of the past, and the groundbreaking scientific achievements of the ancients, had clearly hit a raw nerve deep in the heart of officialdom. That same research may have led to the man's untimely and still-controversial death in a Florida park more than half a century ago. But, 1956 was a prominent year for *additional* government work into the field of gravity manipulation, and it was followed by further official, secret interest in the assertions that the pyramids of Egypt and other huge formations were not created as history, archaeology, and science assures us, as we shall now see.

CONTROLLING GRAVITY

In early January 1956, a British magazine called *Aero Digest* received a clandestine tip-off from a government insider to the effect that officialdom was secretly looking to harness the secrets of gravity for military gain. For two months, *Aero Digest* doggedly and intensively researched the tantalizing tidbits that came its way and ultimately published an article, titled "Anti-gravity Booming," in its March 1956 edition. A.V. Cleaver, commenting on the *Aero Digest* revelations in the *Journal of the British Interplanetary Society*, offered a notable statement: "The Americans have decided to look into the old science-fictional dream of gravity control, or 'anti-gravity,' to investigate, both theoretically and (if possible) practically the fundamental nature of gravitational fields and their relationship to electromagnetic and other phenomena" (Cleaver, 1957).

Clearly, and most importantly, this particular time frame accords very well with that in which elements of the U.S. Navy were interested in learning more about Morris K. Jessup's work in the fields of ancient structures, the Mayans, the Incas, levitation, and gravity manipulation. And things didn't end there. Evidently, *Aero Digest's* writers were the recipients of very solid data: In September 1956, six months after their article appeared, the General Physics Laboratory of the Aeronautical Research Laboratories at Wright-Patterson Air Force Base, Ohio, began *very* quietly studying the nature of gravity and its potential manipulation and control.

Although official documentation on this issue is sorely lacking (actually, it's curiously missing from military archives), it is known that one of those who played a significant role in this project was Joshua N. Goldberg of the department of physics at Syracuse University. And, it seems that, just as was the case with *Aero Digest* in 1956, certain governmental whistleblowers were intent on getting this story out to other media outlets, too. In December 1957, *Product Engineering* noted: "The Air Force is encouraging research in electrogravitics, and many companies and individuals are working on the problem" (*Product Engineering*, 1957).

And as the 1950s became the 1960s, so the gravity-themed research continued—and, once again, matters of a pyramid nature were never very far behind.

A Grid of Power

Bruce Cathie, a now-retired New Zealand–based airline pilot, has presented an interesting theory suggesting that (a) there exists throughout our planet what might be termed a power grid that UFOs, piloted by definitive alien entities, use as a source of energy while traversing the skies of planet Earth; and (b) technology broadly fitting this particular description was also employed in the movement and manipulation of the gigantic blocks that led to the construction of the Egyptian pyramids and numerous other mega-sized stone structures. It was in the late 1960s that Cathie first began to air his views on such matters.

Cathie was absolutely sure it was wholly inconceivable to even imagine that the thousands of stone blocks used in the creation of the various pyramids on our world were fashioned, pulled, and duly hauled into place by nothing more than numerous slaves and workers. And as Cathie rightly noted, the conventional theories for the creation of the pyramids were overwhelmingly beset by major, nearly insurmountable problems. Some of the massive stones used in the creation of the pyramids of Egypt originated in a quarry around 500 miles from where the pyramids stand to this very day. This made Cathie wonder: From where did the huge number of trees come that had to have been chopped down and converted into rollers to transport the stones used to build the pyramids? Certainly, he concluded, not from the barren deserts of Egypt, that's for sure. In Cathie's mind, there was one answer, and one answer only, to explain how the gargantuan stones were moved: by antigravity, which, in simple terms, renders an object free of gravitational force. And it's now that we come to the relationship between Bruce Cathie and the U.S. government.

Anti-gravity in Egypt.
(Copyright Eduard Spetterini, 1904)

The Cathie Files

In the 1960s, when Bruce Cathie's groundbreaking research was coming to fruition, he contacted the U.S. Embassy in New Zealand, chiefly as part of an effort to have his views heard by officialdom, which, Cathie hoped, might assist him in his quest to uncover, and fully understand, the truth about the so-called Earth grid. Interestingly enough, he was duly referred to the Foreign Technology Division (FTD) at Wright-Patterson Air Force Base in Dayton, Ohio, a military base whose role in 1956-era gravity-control research has already been addressed in this chapter, and whose staff was also linked to the Noah's Ark affair.

Stressing that Cathie was a "lean, wiry New Zealander, with an apparently above average knowledge of mathematics," formerly classified U.S. Defense Intelligence Agency, U.S. Army, and Air Force reports of February 1968 and May 1969 reveal that American intelligence agents had secretly undertaken background checks on the man himself. Although the available files on Cathie are scant and incomplete, they do demonstrate that the FTD listened carefully to what Cathie had to say (Walker, 1968).

Moreover, in 1986, Cathie revealed that a Colonel John Burnett of the FTD had invited him to Wright-Patterson where, he was told, intensive, secret research was underway into UFOs on a 24/7 basis. An enthusiastic Cathie was delighted by the invite—which, rather strangely, was then quickly withdrawn. "Perhaps the idea was vetoed in the States," Cathie wondered in correspondence to English UFO authority Timothy Good (Good, 1987).

Secret Surveillance

There is evidence to show that Cathie's digging into such controversial areas as the origins of the pyramids of Egypt, UFO grids, and levitating stones attracted even deeper official attention—and possibly secret surveillance of the man. A now-declassified U.S. Defense Department document of May 1968 references then-recent complaints received from Cathie to the effect that U.S. personnel were secretly tailing him. According to the story that an angry and concerned Cathie told American officials, for some time he had suspected he was being spied upon by stealthy U.S. government agents, but did not receive full vindication of such suspicions until April 1968, when he was accosted in the lobby of the Grand Hotel, Invercargill, New Zealand, by three unidentified Americans. An attempt was made to have Cathie accompany them to locations unknown, which he had the good presence of mind to flatly refuse but which Cathie believed may have been a naval vessel, because he had heard that U.S. Navy personnel were in the area at that very same time.

How curious that the Navy should have popped up in the affairs of both Bruce Cathie and Morris K. Jessup—two researchers open and vocal about their work in the field of anti-gravity. Cathie wasted no time at all in informing the U.S. Department of Defense that his work had been cleared at the highest levels of the government of New Zealand, including by the prime minister. Cathie added to U.S. authorities, in decidedly stern and direct tones: "Call your agents off. I have official approval to continue my work; I don't want them tailing me" (Walker, 1968).

But *someone* continued to take notice: National Security Agency files on Cathie's work are largely comprised of photocopies of pages from his books, from magazines articles, and from book reviews—in other words, open-source literature. Far more intriguing, however, is a memo contained in one particular declassified NSA document on Cathie, of March 1972, that includes the following thought-provoking, and partially redacted, line: "Mr. Cathie's work, theoretical and [two lines deleted] of Von Daniken and the UFO buffs has not gone unnoticed and attention to his continuing work in fields of pyramids and gravity exploitation is being encouraged by several sources for [deleted] at FTD [Foreign Technology Division] and [deleted]" (Callimahos, 1972).

Precisely why Bruce Cathie was put under apparent surveillance by elements of the U.S. Intelligence community is unfortunately, and ultimately, very much unclear. Did he stumble upon the truth behind the UFO controversy and its links to the secrets of how the pyramids of Egypt were really constructed? It's incredibly difficult to say for sure. UFO propulsion systems, long-lost anti-gravity- and levitation-based technology in the hands of the Pharaohs, classified U.S. Department of Defense files, and a covert surveillance operation by the Navy: all key components in the remarkable life and work of Bruce Cathie.

But if the U.S. military did undertake a wealth of research into levitation- and anti-gravity-themed technologies in the 1950s and 1960s, and took at least some of its inspiration from the work of Morris K. Jessup and Bruce Cathie as it related to the construction of ancient pyramids, then why are we not seeing evidence of such technology in widespread use today? Maybe the results are still considered classified and remain locked behind closed doors. In a world dominated and fueled by Middle Eastern oil and large corporations with a lot to lose if new and radical technologies should be made available to one and all, this is understandable—albeit for the rest of us very regrettable, too. Such a scenario is not impossible.

A retired Marine Corps major, Donald E. Keyhoe, noted that research into gravity control seemed to fall under the auspices of the military and, more importantly, the domain of official secrecy. Commenting, in 1974, on the U.S. Air Force's early work in the field of gravity control and gravity-manipulation, Keyhoe said: "When AF [Air Force] researchers fully realized the astounding possibilities, headquarters persuaded scientists, aerospace companies and technical laboratories to set up anti-gravity projects, many of them under secret contracts. Every year, the number of projects increased" (Keyhoe, 1974).

As far back as 1965, Keyhoe revealed, he had knowledge of 46 programs linked to gravity-based research, of which more than 30 fell under the jurisdiction of the Air Force. As with Las Vegas, when it comes to anti-gravity, it seems that what happens in the military stays in the military. If the U.S. government *has* secretly figured out how the pyramids of eras and civilizations long-gone were really constructed—and there is a realization, or a nagging suspicion, that it involved manifestly incredible and alternative technologies that had the manipulation of gravity at their heart—it appears hell-bent on keeping the rest of us in the dark. And in relation to the story of Morris K. Jessup, it may have resorted to cold-blooded murder to protect its secrets. The gravity of the situation (in every sense of the word) may be more than we can scarcely begin to imagine.

ANCIENT ATOMIC ANNIHILATION

The idea that, thousands of years in the past, there may have existed highly technologically advanced societies that understood, and duly harnessed, atomic energy (to the point where they all but eventually destroyed themselves) sounds controversial in the extreme. Amazingly, however, such an inflammatory scenario cannot be ruled out. Nor we can we rule out the possibility that one of the foremost players in the U.S. government's very own 1940s-era program to utilize the atom as a weapon possessed secret, archaic knowledge on this very matter. The man in question, none other than the legendary J. Robert Oppenheimer, may have dropped subtle hints about that same knowledge, on at least several occasions, that civilizations rose long before ours and fell as a result of their reckless use, and misuse, of atomic power. The strange saga dates back to the earliest days of Indian culture and civilization, in which there exists a particularly important collection of material that tells fascinating stories of the nation's early cultures, kingdoms, ways of life, and catastrophic warfare. It is one of the mightiest of all Sanskrit tomes. It is called the *Mahabharata*.

Battle Looms

Along with the *Ramayana*, the *Mahabharata* is acknowledged by Indian scholars as representing the most significant of all the ancient Sanskrit texts that chronicle the tales of this vastly old nation, its people, its history, and its wars—specifically on this latter point, the Kurukshetra War, which occurred in what is today the northern Indian state of Haryana. As for when the war took place, some researchers of the *Mahabharata* suggest possibly as early as 8,000 years ago and perhaps even significantly before that date. As we shall see, however, this was no normal war waged with such ancient weaponry as spears and bows and arrows. Quite the opposite: It may have been a conflict ignited by nothing less than the destructive power of the atom.

As the *Mahabharata* tells it, at the time of the Kurukshetra War, there existed an Indo-Aryan culture in northern India known as the Kuru. It flourished during the Vedic period, when the very oldest of all Hindu scriptures, the Vedas, were first set down. Within this culture were two powerful, competing, and connected groups: They were the Kauravas (which translates as the descendants of Kuru) and the Pandavas, so named after King Pandu, who ruled

Hastinapur in the northern part of India. Hastinapur also happened to be the capital of the kingdom of the Kauravas people. Bitter rivalry, ever-present turf wars, and the regular flexing of military muscles were very much the order of the day, as both sought to exert their power and control over the entire area.

Matters eventually came to an irreversible and cataclysmic butting of heads when an all-out, 18-day-long military confrontation erupted: the Kurukshetra War. For the victor, the prize was huge territories, masses of people, and myriad ancient and exotic towns and cities. Recognizing the significance of the rapidly escalating situation, other Indian armies and kings scrambled to align themselves with whomever they perceived as being the potential victor. What had begun as a series of mild skirmishes and quarrels was now much more. And it all ended in sudden, all-destructive death from the skies.

Some scholars view the *Mahabharata* as having been written in decidedly fanciful and exaggerated style—myth, folklore, and legend, for all intents and purposes. In recent years, however, this priceless piece of work has become the subject of a great deal of study by those fascinated by the mysteries of ancient civilizations whose times have long since evaporated. The reason why is as simple as it is almost unbelievable and inconceivable: Many of the texts contained within the *Mahabharata* can, by our standards today, be interpreted as graphic depictions of nothing less than all-out, ancient nuclear war and its terrible side effects of radiation poisoning and massive destruction.

Skeptics may scoff, but none can deny the powerful words of the *Mahabharata* that are highly suggestive of

Was atomic war fought in ancient India?
(Copyright U.S. Dept. of Energy)

atomic secrets known, and utilized, in antiquity. One notable section chillingly details what sounds like the unleashing and detonation of an atomic weapon at the height of
battle. The translated version describes a nightmarish scene:
A rain of fiery arrows descended from the skies, waters
boiled, the very Earth itself shuddered, the Sun appeared

to shake in the sky, and untold numbers of soldiers were killed in a terrifying inferno from above. Interestingly, the *Mahabharata* also tells of how, in the immediate years after this terrible war, the heavens remained permanently dark as a result of thick, unmoving clouds that blocked out the Sun. This is very akin to the so-called Nuclear Winter scenario that has been suggested might befall our civilization following a significantly sized nuclear exchange between the superpowers.

Top Guns of the Past

Also of deep interest: The *Mahabharata* records incredible battles fought in the skies of India during the Kurukshetra War by skilled pilots using what were termed Vimanas. But from their description, they sound just like highly advanced equivalents of today's military jet-fighters, capable of flying at fantastic speeds and heights, and targeting the enemy with weapons possibly of a nuclear nature.

One such ancient account of apparent atomic weapons unleashed from a Vimana during the Kurukshetra War reads as follows: "Gurkha, flying in his swift and powerful Vimana, hurled against the three cities of the Vrishnis and Andhakas a single projectile charged with all the power of the Universe. An incandescent column of smoke and fire, as brilliant as ten thousand suns, rose in all its splendor. It was the unknown weapon, the iron thunderbolt, a gigantic messenger of death" (Majimdar, 1951).

Furthermore, this devastating weapon from above specifically poisoned food, made people's hair and nails fall out, and led troops to throw themselves into streams and rivers to try to decontaminate themselves. Researcher Rene Noorbergen, who closely studied the issue of ancient nuclear warfare in India, noted the old descriptions were "unnervingly similar" to what has been reported in our very own atomic explosions (Noorbergen, 2001).

Interestingly, Colonel Henry S. Olcott, the co-founder with Helen Blavatsky and William Quan Judge of the Theosophical Society (the original mandate of which was the study and elucidation of occultism) said: "The ancient Hindus could navigate the air, and not only navigate it, but fight battles in it like so many war-eagles combating for the domination of the clouds. To be so perfect in aeronautics, they must have known all the arts and sciences related to [aeronautics], including the strata and currents of the atmosphere, the relative temperature, humidity, density and specific gravity of the various gases" (Olcott, 1881).

Similarly, Professor Ramchandra Dikshitar, of Madras University, spelled out his views on such issues: "No question can be more interesting in the present circumstance of the world than India's contribution to the science of aeronautics. There are numerous illustrations in our vast Puranic and epic literature to show how well and wonderfully the ancient Indians conquered the air" (Dikshitar, 1944).

So, if the Vimanas were real, what was the nature of the incredible technology involved in their construction and deployment? The Sanskrit *Samarangana Sutradhara*, written in the 11th century by King Raja Bhoja, who ruled in Malwa, India, said of the Vimana that they should be strong, durable, light, and powered by an engine of mercury. This, the old records stated, would allow the pilot to take the craft high into the sky and travel at incredible speeds and immense distances, as well as even fly vertically and backward.

Of deep relevance to this matter of a mercury-powered Vimana, Henry Monteith, who worked at the New Mexico–based Sandia Laboratories, noted that gasified mercury would make a highly efficient turbine propellant. Ancient mysteries researcher Richard Wingate has gone on record as stating that Monteith, who has taken an interest in UFOs, psychic phenomena, cosmology, and the curious phenomenon of cattle mutilations, among many other topics, is "convinced that the Indian engineers had actually built a Vimana." When Wingate asked Monteith, who worked on a number of classified, U.S. military programs, if "we were making such craft today somewhere on earth," Monteith preferred not to answer the question (Wingate, 2011).

None need to be told that even the very notion of war having been waged thousands of years ago with atomic weapons and fighter planes flies in the face of absolutely everything that history and archaeology hold dear. But, that the *Mahabharata* and the *Samarangana Sutradhara* possibly tell us otherwise, suggests we may want to reconsider the notion of whether or not we really are the first civilization on this planet to have harnessed atomic energy. Are we, perhaps, just the latest in a line—maybe even in a *long* line—of people who have come to understand the atom, but who are ultimately—and, possibly, given our warlike nature, *always*—destined to use it as a tool of widespread destruction and complete downfall? These are questions that, incredibly, certain individuals attached to the most classified program of World War II (the Manhattan Project, which saw the development of the atomic bombs that leveled Japan in 1945) may secretly have known a good deal about.

Oppenheimer's Secrets

Beyond any shadow of doubt, it was the harnessing of atomic energy that brought World War II to a decisive and destructive end when the Japanese cities of Hiroshima and Nagasaki were decimated by U.S.–built and –deployed atomic weapons. The former was bombed on August 6, 1945, and the latter three days later. The scale of death and destruction was shocking, even to those who viewed the actions as justified, given the many atrocities that the Japanese military carried out against Allied troops during the war. At Hiroshima, the death toll reached well into six figures, and at Nagasaki estimates suggest around 80,000 people lost their lives—the vast majority being civilians, rather than members of the Japanese armed forces.

Not surprisingly, faced with the potential, steady, step-by-step, complete obliteration of Japan and its people, Japan's Emperor Hirohito announced the nation's surrender on August 15th. But, as peace returned to rest of the world, Japan was faced with rebuilding a ravaged and scarred landscape, and dealing with the loss of hundreds of thousands of people, and tens of thousands seriously injured, irradiated individuals. Even though the actions of U.S. President Harry S. Truman ensured much-needed world peace, the scale of terror and horror that swept across the planet when the incredible might of the atom became graphically realized brought calls for atomic weapons never, ever to be used in battle again, and, so far they have not. But, it's what came *after* the bombing of Japan that is particularly intriguing.

Robert Oppenheimer, who was fascinated by Mahabharata. (Copyright U.S. Dept. of Energy.)

Within the realm of atomic research and the development of the bomb, no name is more well-known than that of Robert Oppenheimer. Born in 1904, Oppenheimer was a theoretical physicist and was employed as a professor of physics at the Berkeley-based University of California. Referred to as the father of the atomic bomb, Oppenheimer was a leading figure in the top secret, World War II–era Manhattan Project that developed the first atomic weapon.

His place in history is well and truly assured. But, just like a number of his colleagues, Oppenheimer was deeply shocked—and profoundly psychologically scarred and altered—by the sheer scale of destruction and death that his creations wrought upon Japan and its people. Just like Mary Shelley's fictional Dr. Victor Frankenstein, Oppenheimer, too, came to rue the day that his very own monster was let loose upon an unsuspecting world.

As a result, Oppenheimer (to the complete annoyance of the U.S. government) became an outspoken champion of the idea that the development and use of atomic weaponry should be curtailed and kept in constant check. With the Cold War escalating, and with widespread fears of a nuclear confrontation with the Soviets growing, this was most certainly not what the U.S. military, the CIA, the FBI, and just about every other arm of officialdom wished to hear, and particularly not from the very brains behind the bomb. Coupled with the fact that the government suspected he had dabbled in communism from time to time, Oppenheimer, in 1954, was relieved of his security clearance and was summarily ejected from the elite, secret world that he had so dominated at the height of World War II.

Oppenheimer might have lost his clearance to the insider secrets of atomic research, but he had some choice and intriguing words to say about the U.S. development of the atomic bomb. And many of those words harked right back to the tales of the *Mahabharata*.

"I Am Become Death"

Just 48 hours before the first, secret, testing of an atomic bomb at the White Sands Proving Ground in Alamogordo, New Mexico, on July 16, 1945, Oppenheimer felt prompted to ponder upon a particular quotation from an Indian text, the *Bhagavad Gita*, a 700-verse scripture contained within the *Mahabharata* itself. When the war was over, he revealed those words: "In battle, in the forest, at the precipice in the mountains, on the dark great sea, in the midst of javelins and arrows, in sleep, in confusion, in the depths of shame, the good deeds a man has done before defend him" (Majimdar, 1951).

After the atomic bombing of Japan in August 1945, Oppenheimer reflected: "We knew the world would not be the same. A few people laughed, a few people cried, most people were silent. I remembered the line from the Hindu scripture, the *Bhagavad Gita*. Vishnu is trying to persuade the Prince that he should do his duty and to impress him takes on his multi-armed form and says, 'Now, I am become Death, the destroyer of worlds.' I suppose we all thought that one way or another" (J. Robert Oppenheimer, "Now I am become death...," 1965).

Much of the content of the *Bhagavad Gita* is focused upon a conversation that took place between Lord Krishna and the Arjuna, a Pandava prince. It was right at the time the Kurukshetra War was about to break out, and when just about all diplomatic attempts to avert disaster and head-to-head confrontation had miserably failed. The *Bhagavad Gita* is filled with stories of terrifying weapons fired upon one another by opposing forces. And Oppenheimer, for reasons tantalizingly unknown, felt compelled to note this publicly. In fact, he did so on numerous occasions, and for years, when he was questioned about atomic weaponry.

We should also note the words of Isidor Rabi, who was a physicist, friend, and colleague of Oppenheimer, and someone who also worked on the Manhattan Project. Rabi, who ultimately went on to become a science advisor to President Harry S. Truman and a Nobel Prize–winner in the field of physics, said of Oppenheimer that he was "overeducated in those fields which lie outside the scientific tradition, such as his interest in religion, in the Hindu religion in particular, which resulted in a feeling of mystery of the universe that surrounded him like a fog." Rabi added that Oppenheimer moved away from "the hard, crude methods of theoretical physics into a mystical realm of broad intuition" (Rhodes, 1986).

"Yes, It Was the First One—in Modern Times, of Course."

There is a highly significant statement Oppenheimer made in 1952, while attending a conference on atomic weapons research at the University of Rochester, New York. During a question-and-answer session, Oppenheimer was asked by an attendee if the atomic weapon exploded in 1945 at Alamogordo, New Mexico, during the Trinity Project, was the first one ever to be detonated. A somewhat-startled Oppenheimer replied after a couple of seconds: "Yes, it was the first one." Then, after yet a further moment or two of hesitation, he added: "In modern times, of course." A curious five-word statement, to say the least. Perhaps, privately, having intensively studied and quoted the *Mahabharata*, Oppenheimer came to believe that ours is not the first highly advanced culture to have populated the Earth, or the first to have felt the thunderous and devastating effects of atomic warfare (Oppenheimer, 1954).

After contracting throat cancer, Robert Oppenheimer died on February 18, 1967. He took with him to the grave any and all secrets he may have possessed relative to his fascination with the *Mahabharata* and his comments made in 1952 concerning ancient atomic-driven annihilation.

Notably, *another* renowned scientist, Frederick Soddy, who was championed for his contributions in the field of the chemistry of radioactive substances, was also deeply conversant with the *Mahabharata*. The English scientist, who died in 1956, two years after Oppenheimer lost his security clearance, wrote in his book, *The Interpretation of Radium*, that with respect to the words of the *Mahabharata*: "Can we not read in them some justification for the belief that some former forgotten race of men attained not only to the knowledge we have so recently won, but also to the power that is not yet ours?" (Soddy, 1912)

Soddy continued, in quite remarkable tones: "I believe that there have been civilizations in the past that were familiar with atomic energy, and that by misusing it they were totally destroyed" (Ibid.).

Is it just coincidence that two scientists (Oppenheimer and Soddy) very familiar with the *Mahabharata*, both made comments, the former somewhat enigmatic and the latter very openly, about the use of atomic weaponry in the distant past? Or, did the exposure of both men to the world of official secrecy and skullduggery reveal to them dark, arcane government knowledge of cultures and people obliterated by their own science? And did Oppenheimer's latter-day fears about the use and misuse of atomic weapons stem from his secret knowledge that we were in deep and dire danger of repeating what certain Indian cultures had done thousands of years earlier?

Perhaps, in his own alternative and roundabout way, Oppenheimer was trying to reveal to us top secrets that he felt uncomfortable discussing openly to the fullest degree. Maybe we should listen to his words. The Cold War is over, but the War on Terror is not. And, the sheer number of atomic warheads in the hands of numerous nations still has the ability to carve a new, terrifying world of mega-death and nuclear nightmare in mere minutes. If we choose to ignore Oppenheimer's warnings and comments, we may see the day when our culture meets its end in a fiery, radioactive inferno, possibly just like that of the mysterious, powerful people of the *Mahabharata* all those thousands of years ago.

TALK LIKE
AN EGYPTIAN

Early ESP

Born Henry Puharich in 1918, Andrija Puharich was an American of Yugoslavian descent who, from the late 1940s in a laboratory in Glen Cove, Maine, called the Round Table Foundation, became fascinated by the realm of extra-sensory perception (ESP), and spent much of his life trying to understand the nature of the phenomenon, and unraveling its many and varied complexities. In addition, Puharich had significant links to officialdom. He was a captain in the U.S. Army and, from 1953 to 1955, worked at and closely liaised with a number of prestigious figures from the Edgewood, Maryland–based Army Chemical Center.

Thus, it wasn't long before the government began to take an interest in Puharich's studies into the wild and churning mysteries of the human mind, even more so when those same studies spilled over into the realm of ancient Egypt.

From 1947 onward, Puharich worked diligently to penetrate the domain of ESP, but it was not until August 1952 that matters really began to heat up. During that particular month Puharich received a curious visit from a high-ranking source within the Army. At first glance, the visit seemed wholly innocent: The man in question was an old friend and colleague of Puharich, and it appeared he had just turned up for a friendly chat. Maybe he had, but that was most certainly not all he was there for. It did not take Puharich's friend any time at all to turn the seemingly casual conversation around to a discussion of Puharich's expanding work in the realm of ESP. Nor did it take Puharich's buddy long to stress to him that the Army would like to be kept informed of any aspects of his work that could potentially be militarized, due to the Pentagon being particularly intrigued by his studies.

By November 1952, Puharich had discovered something startling: The ability of a person to exhibit and successfully utilize ESP was significantly increased when that same person was placed inside a Faraday cage. An invention of an English physicist, Michael Faraday, a Faraday cage essentially blocks electric fields, similar to the means by which electronic equipment and buildings can be protected from powerful lightning strikes. This discovery struck a deep chord with the Army, who invited Puharich to Washington, D.C., to deliver a lecture on ESP to high-ranking Pentagon personnel. He did so, and to great interest, on November 24, 1952.

The time frame of Puharich's research was highly important: It coincided with the early years of the U.S. government's secret and controversial research into psychedelic drugs, hypnosis, and psychological manipulation or, mind control, in simple-yet-stark terminology. Much of this work was undertaken under the banner of the CIA's now-notorious MK-Ultra program, a clandestine operation that operated out of the CIA's Office of Scientific Intelligence and that had its beginnings in the Cold War era of the late 1940s and very early 1950s.

To demonstrate the level of secrecy that surrounded Project MK-Ultra, even though it had kicked off years before, its existence was largely unknown outside of the intelligence world until 1975, when the Church Committee and the Rockefeller Commission began making their own independent investigations of the CIA's mind-control-related activities. The story that unfolded was filled to the brim with controversy. The scope of the project was spelled out in an August 1977 document titled *The Senate MK-Ultra Hearings* that was prepared by the Senate Select Committee on Intelligence and the Committee on Human Resources, as a result of its probing into the secret and dark world of the CIA.

The author of the document explained: "Research and development programs to find materials which could be used to alter human behavior were initiated in the late 1940s and early 1950s. These experimental programs originally included testing of drugs involving witting human subjects, and culminated in tests using unwitting, non-volunteer human subjects. These tests were designed to determine the potential effects of chemical or biological agents when used operationally against individuals unaware that they had received a drug" (Senate Select Committee, 1977).

The Committee was highly concerned to learn that with respect to the mind-control and mind-manipulation projects, the CIA's normal administrative controls were controversially waived for programs involving chemical and biological agents supposedly to protect their security, but more likely to protect those CIA personnel who knew they were coming precariously close to breaking the law. What the Committee was not overly familiar with at the time, however, were various sub-projects under the overall MK-Ultra banner that were following winding pathways similar to Puharich's work. One of them, almost unbelievably, involved something that extended way back to the early years of ancient Egypt, no less.

Mushrooms, Shaman, and Secret Agents

Of those individuals who claimed extraordinary ESP-based abilities, and who Puharich spent a great deal of time studying in the 1950s, one was a man named Harry Stone, a Dutch sculptor who, on a variety of occasions, reportedly and spontaneously entered trance states, in which he both spoke and wrote in Egyptian. Even more controversially, while in those same altered states, Stone's personality was allegedly taken over by that of a long-dead Egyptian prince, Rahotep. Whether Stone was channeling Rahotep, or had actually *been* Rahotep in a previous incarnation, was an issue of ongoing debate. But there was far more. In addition to divulging a fascinating and varied body of data on the world and the era of the Pharaohs, Stone/Rahotep revealed to Puharich that central to the ability to exist, travel, and manifest in astral form was *Amanita Muscaria*—something that has since become known as the Sacred Mushroom.

Amanita Muscaria is a psychoactive fungus that can have extreme effects upon the human body and mind, even to the point of provoking extraordinary visionary experiences. Conventional science and medicine prefer to consider such visions as being purely internal to the percipient and having no tangible reality outside of the confines of the human mind. Puharich, however, came to believe that this definitively magic mushroom quite literally allowed for astral travel, out-of-body experiences, and possibly even the ability to traverse not just to other, far more ethereal realms of existence, but maybe even through the very barriers of time itself.

If one knew how to carefully harness the power of *Amanita Muscaria* one could, perhaps, take a trip to the early days of Egypt—or to just about anywhere one desired. And it almost seemed that higher forces of a supernatural, non-human nature were positively manipulating Puharich's every move: He stumbled upon a fine specimen of *Amanita Muscaria* only 1 mile from his very own laboratory. Coincidence, in the mind of Puharich, this most assuredly was not. The guiding hand of something far stranger than mere chance had descended upon Glen Cove.

It is hardly surprising that all of this became of extensive interest to the CIA. After all, imagine the ultimate scenario: Instead of having to secretly dispatch its agents to the Kremlin to uncover the Soviet Union's latest developments in the field of atomic weaponry, the CIA could instead train those same agents—via the ingestion of *Amanita Muscaria*—to travel astrally to Russia and secure all the data needed by extraordinary mind-power, rather than risk them having to physically break into secure, well-guarded vaults deep below the city of Moscow. The CIA, by this time, was already heavily involved in LSD-based research, so feeding a few mushrooms to a secret assortment of volunteers, guinea-pigs, and unwitting test subjects, was hardly perceived as being overly controversial or hazardous an action.

This is precisely what took place at CIA HQ and deep in the heart of several East Coast universities and hospitals that had agreed to secretly perform such controversial experimentation for the CIA. The barriers of the mind were broken down, and *secret* agents were duly transformed into *shamanic* agents, spying on the enemy via methods very old, extremely archaic, infinitely weird, and not even precisely understood. But, for the CIA, the important thing was that (at times, anyway) those same mysterious methods seemed to work for their personnel in much the same way they were massively shaping the research and world of Puharich.

Tripping Into the Past

CIA documentation on this particular matter is extremely limited and heavily redacted. Nevertheless, we can glean a few extraordinary nuggets of data from the presently available material. At least as far back as October 1953—which actually predates some of Puharich's more significant work, and suggests he was not the only source who put the Agency on the trail of the secrets of mushrooms and the mind—the CIA was already tentatively dabbling into the mysteries of *Amanita Muscaria*.

A number of the available files refer to unfortunate physical and psychological side effects reported by some of those who were new to the powers of the Sacred Mushroom, such as nausea, vomiting, panic attacks, and claustrophobia. This is not at all unusual. As the CIA came to learn, and as most users of psychedelics will be fully aware, when it comes to undergoing a trip of the mind kind, the setting and the mood are equally as important as the substance itself. Thus, if the trip occurs in sterile surroundings, filled with stern agents of the CIA looking like they just strode off the set of Hollywood's *Men in Black*, the trip may prove to be an eventful one, but of a non-relaxed, traumatic, and negative nature. When the participant is open and receptive to whatever may be just around the corner and without any form of outside intimidation or influence playing a role, the effect can be much different, very pleasant, and extremely mind-expanding.

One particular CIA document, of March 1956, refers to an experiment on "Subject 16, Aberdeen, V77" who, according to the CIA, while tripping on *Amanita Muscaria*, reported "a fanciful 'journey' to Egyptian Pyramids and told of sighting 'flying stones' and 'flying saucers.'" The writer of the report added: "If this is the limit of what we can expect to see from [the use of *Amanita Muscaria*] then we should reconsider [the remainder deleted]." Clearly, whoever prepared this particular partially censored report was hardly impressed, and perceived the results achieved to be little more than induced fantasies and not much else. However, the time frame (the mid to late 1950s) and the scenario of "flying stones" that were used to construct the pyramids of Egypt, are eerily reminiscent of the stories of Morris K. Jessup, whose work in the field of Egyptian levitation was of deep interest to the U.S. Navy during this very same time frame (Central Intelligence Agency, 1956).

Celebrity Psychics and the CIA

Another CIA report from 1959 refers to a participant in the *Amanita Muscaria* program who, after several mushroom-based journeys into the unknown, had inexplicably become fixated on famous psychics Jeane Dixon and Ruth Montgomery, the latter also being a prominent journalist. Notably, Montgomery had published a story Dixon told that was both fascinating and Egyptian-themed, and that also attracted CIA attention.

On June 14, 1960, Ruth Montgomery splashed an article on government research into ESP across the pages of the *New York Journal American* newspaper. Its title was "Spying by Mind-Reading." It strongly suggested someone in officialdom had given Montgomery an off-the-record briefing on the CIA's magic mushroom–themed program. In fact, it was Montgomery's revelations in the *Journal* that led legendary FBI head honcho, J. Edgar Hoover to ask if there was anything concrete to the story. Hoover did so in a memo sent to three of the FBI's most respected and powerful figures: Clyde Tolson, the FBI's associate director; Alan Belmont, assistant director of the Domestic Intelligence Division of the FBI; and Cartha DeLoach, who in 1948 became the liaison point between the FBI and the CIA. Intriguingly, although initially Hoover was told that the claims made in Montgomery's article had absolutely no merit to them, Army Intelligence and the CIA soon thereafter radically altered their position to Hoover and admitted to having undertaken such experimentation, but with results described as being mixed, which is hardly a denial of at least *some* positive results.

As for Jeane Dixon, she was a psychic whose allure was so powerful that it influenced the mindsets and actions of two U.S. presidents: Richard Nixon and Ronald Reagan. As for the former, in 1972 he established a committee on terrorism after Dixon prophesized a wave of terrorist attacks on U.S. soil. First Lady Nancy Regan was an avid follower of Dixon's teachings. She made sure that the president himself listened very carefully to what Dixon had to say.

Nailing the Nine

As for Puharich, his story was elevated to even higher levels of strangeness. One of those whose experiences and talents that Puharich was intrigued by, in the early 1950s, was Dr. D.G. Vinod, a definitive mystic from India who claimed the ability to channel what became known as the Nine Principles, or just the Nine. The reason for the name was simple: The Nine represented the primary deities of Egypt comprised of the god Atum, and under him, his nine children: Set, Osiris, Shu, Tefnut, Geb, Horus, Isis, Nepthys, and Nut, who were worshipped at Heliopolis, the City of the Sun, located just east of the River Nile. The Nine, however, claimed they, the Ennead, were actually ancient aliens from the Sirius star-system who seeded humanity in Tibet around 32,400 BC.

From there, things became even more controversial. In 1971, Puharich hooked up with none other than Uri Geller, who was on the verge of becoming world-famous—or, maybe, world-infamous. In 1971, Puharich met with Geller in Tel Aviv and hypnotized him. The reason was to try to understand the point of origin for Geller's alleged extraordinary psychic skills. According to the story, what happened next is that Geller began to channel messages from a sentient computer-based intelligence of alien origins known as Spectra. Notably, Puharich suggested that Spectra might actually have been one of the legendary Nine. Lo and behold, Spectra quickly agreed that he, she, or it was indeed one of the Nine. How convenient. Geller had the Nine to thank for all his amazing, psychic skills. And the world would soon come to know it, too.

But who, exactly, were the Nine? On this particular matter, the investigative team of Lynne Picknett and Clive Prince noted Puharich appeared to have a distinctly sinister side. The pair revealed that Puharich had studied a number of ways to alter or provoke certain thought processes, "even to creating the impression of voices in the head." These particular skills included the use of "drugs, hypnosis and beaming radio signals directly into the subject's brain." Picknett and Prince added that Puharich's work in this particularly controversial arena was performed at the same time the Nine made their debut at Glen Cove. With that in mind, everyone should take careful note of the next words from Picknett and Prince concerning Puharich's Round Table Foundation: "The Foundation itself is now known to have been largely funded by the Pentagon as a front for its medical and parapsychological research. Puharich was still working for the CIA in the early 1970s, when he brought Uri Geller out of Israel" (Picknett and Prince, 2002).

The Nine seemed to have been distinctly racist, too, and suggested that all races on planet Earth are the result of intervention by space-gods—all, that is, except for one: the black race, which the Nine claimed do not hold such lofty distinction. The clear, and utterly outrageous, implication is that the white man is superior to the black man because the former was the creation of superior beings from beyond the Earth and the latter was not. And how do we know this? Ancient aliens from Sirius—the Nine—have told us so, because they deigned and designed it exactly that way!

The thought-provoking opinion of Picknett and Prince is that, perhaps, the Nine originated not in some faraway solar system, but within the heart of a CIA program designed to achieve the enslavement and manipulation of the human mind. The reason: to take control of the New Age movement. The pair correctly noted that with respect to that same movement, "it would be a mistake to underestimate the economic or even political potential of this vast subculture" (Ibid.).

And maybe, if the shocking scenario is true, some of those behind the creation and promulgation of the Nine's ideology were distinct racists, too, intent on trying to make the white race the dominating force on planet Earth. As possible evidence of the CIA's outright creation of—or, at the absolute very least, significant manipulation of— the mythos of the Nine, we see that the Nine hate Islam. Muslims, the Nine confidently assure us, are the children of darkness.

The Temple of Sirius

Finally, there is one other issue that also links the CIA with tales of ancient aliens from Sirius, which, just like the Puharich/Geller saga, also surfaced in the 1970s. Published in 1976, Robert Temple's book, *The Sirius Mystery*, detailed a fantastic story that captured the imaginations of the public and the media en masse when it was first released. That story, which Temple had been working on diligently and devotedly since 1967, told of very ancient visitations by extra-terrestrials based in the Sirius star-system to the Dogon people, who make their home near the city of Bandiagara, Africa.

In 1998, Temple's book was republished with a considerable amount of new material contained therein. One of the many revelations of the expanded version of *The Sirius Mystery* was that in the immediate aftermath of the publication of the original edition 22 years earlier, the author found himself watched closely by elements of both American and British Intelligence. Temple incurred the wrath of certain sources within NASA. He learned from retired brigadier Shelford Bidwell that he became a subject of interest to the British security services, a claim that was bolstered by the words of a friend of Temple, who had been "approached by MI5 [the British equivalent of the FBI] to do a security report on me." And, Temple told of attempts by the CIA to prevent him from joining the Foreign Press Association. Somewhere during the course of his research into the Sirius-Dogon connection Temple had hit upon a distinctly raw and conspiratorial nerve (Temple, 1998).

Given that the collective New Age movement is a huge one, is it really too extreme to imagine that the CIA may have wanted to influence both it and its followers—massive in number and planet-wide in scope—as a means to control and manipulate Western society's belief systems of an esoteric nature? Maybe the CIA's interest in such characters as Jeane Dixon and Ruth Montgomery was not because of what they might have discovered relative to ancient Egypt. Perhaps the surveillance was undertaken to try to determine how successfully the CIA's faked stories of ancient aliens, and its MK-Ultra-style mind manipulations relative to possibly bogus outer-space-linked issues such as the Nine, were pulling the strings of the New Age arena.

RED PLANET
MYSTERIES

Cydonia's Secrets

Situated in a region of the planet Mars called Cydonia is a curious and immense structure that has become famous within the fields of astronomy, planetary exploration, and conspiracy theorizing. Around 1 mile in length and half a mile in width, it is known as the Face on Mars. For NASA's public affairs people, the massive visage is nothing more than the result of a definitive piece of pareidolia, the process by which the human brain can interpret random imagery as having some meaning or significance behind it. A classic example being the way in which, at one time or another, most of us have seen faces in clouds.

But, is pareidolia really all that is behind the Face on Mars, as NASA states publicly? Or is there something stranger going on? Might the Face on Mars actually be one of the few remaining remnants of an ancient Martian culture that vanished in planet-wide catastrophe millennia ago? And, even more controversially, what of the claims of some figures within the Face on Mars research community who suspect that the giant structure is somehow connected to the pyramids and Sphinx of Egypt? To answer those questions, let's go back to July 25, 1976, when the massive creation—whether of nature or of Martians—was first photographed by NASA's *Viking 1* spacecraft.

The Face in Mars: The work of long-extinct Martians? (Copyright NASA.)

A Trick of the Light?

Mac Tonnies was the author of *After the Martian Apocalypse*, which discusses the Face on Mars. Tonnies came to believe that the controversy-filled structure probably *did* have artificial origins and was *not* simply a natural oddity. And he had good reasons for reaching such a conclusion, too. The initial image of the Face taken by *Viking 1*, which has since become instantly recognizable the world over, did not stand alone. A second photograph was secured by NASA on that same *Viking* mission that added extra weight to the idea that the Face on Mars potentially represented something profoundly unusual and unnatural. This was hardly good news for NASA, which clearly recognized the inevitable controversy the pictures would generate at a public level and which ultimately sought to play down the matter by flying the flag of pareidolia.

Of that second image, specifically frame 70A13, Tonnies noted that, rather than disputing the face-like appearance of the first, it actually advanced the idea that the structure did indeed eerily resemble a human-like face: "Taken at a more revealing sun-angle than its predecessor, Viking frame 70A13 showed a continuation of the 'mouth' feature and, despite apparent odds, a second 'eye.'" And as Tonnies also commented, if the facial likeness was merely an illusion, "why does it persist in more recent images? One would rightly expect a natural surface formation to look less like a face when seen in high resolution" (Redfern, 2004).

As for those claims of nothing more than pareidolia being responsible for the excitement born out of the July 1976, *Viking 1* pictures, Tonnies commented thus: "Mainstream skeptics commonly dismiss the Face on Mars. Most of the likenesses described by Face on Mars debunkers are profile images. Viewed from only a slightly different angle, the celebrated face-like resemblance vanishes, replaced by an obviously natural phenomenon. While profiles rely on a minimum of information to convey a sense of the mysterious—contours to suggest features such as a 'nose,' 'mouth,' etc.—the Face on Mars is different in several notable respects. For instance, the Face appears to be a frontal portrait. While computer modeling reveals a striking facial profile when seen from the perspective of an observer on the Martian surface, the Face retains a humanoid likeness when viewed from above. This doesn't prove that the Face is the work of intelligence, but it tends to elevate it from the oft mentioned examples wielded by geologists convinced the Face on Mars must invariably yield to prosaic explanations" (Ibid.).

Global Odysseys

Photographic evidence that was obtained by NASA's Mars Global Surveyor craft in both 1998 and 2001, and by the Mars *Odyssey* probe one year later, disillusioned many that had earlier promoted the idea that the Face was an ancient artificial construction. If it *was* a face, it now looked like one that one that had just gone through a car windshield at 100 mph. Inevitably, and maybe with a great deal of justifiable reasoning, too, conspiracy theorists quickly asserted that shadowy figures within NASA had deliberately altered the photos. Years later, the controversy still continues.

On the matter of these latter-day photos, Mac Tonnies revealed: "High-resolution images of the Face reveal detail not visible in the early Viking photographs. Astronomer Tom Van Flandern, for instance, quickly noted the presence of accurately situated features such as an apparent 'pupil' in one of the 'eyes;' as well as 'nostrils' and 'lips'—all of which were beyond the resolving power of the Viking mission. The low odds of such secondary facial characteristics occurring by chance helped belie the notion that the Face on Mars was the product of garden variety pareidolia. If the Face on Mars is indeed a windblown butte, it's a great deal stranger than imagined prior to high-resolution scans. Indeed, if the same level of detail had been detected on a terrestrial surface feature, it's probable that archaeologists would have been consulted in order to assess its merit as a potential artifact" (Ibid.).

Tonnies had much more he wanted to get off his chest, too: "When the face was reimaged [by NASA] in 1998, debunkers condescendingly noted the lack of 'roads' and parked 'flying saucers' that would conclusively demonstrate artificiality. But given Mars' age and geological history, superficial features like 'roads' would be the last things one might reasonably expect to find; unless, of course, Mars was home to an active alien civilization with a penchant for terrestrial architecture (Redfern, 2006).

"The fact that virtually no one seriously considered Mars to be home to an extant civilization was brushed aside to accommodate the skeptical community's need to shoot down the looming myth that the Face has become in the decades since it was first photographed. Sadly, the opportunity to address the issue of extra-terrestrial archaeology in scientific terms was squandered, leaving a residue of misconceptions that only fueled the 'fringe's' obsession with conspiracy theories (Ibid.).

"Long before the Mars Global Surveyor spacecraft returned provocative images of the Cydonia Mensae region of Mars, the presence of secondary facial characteristics had been predicted by proponents of what became known as the Artificiality Hypothesis. It seemed likely that the Face, if the work of intelligence, would betray traces of anthropomorphic detail when imaged by better cameras. The 'eye' was only barely visible in the best of the early Viking photos from the 1970s; certainly little or nothing about its shape or structure could be inferred (Ibid.).

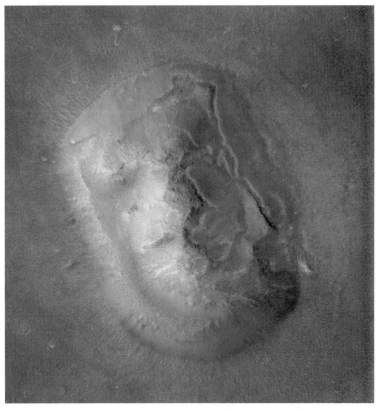

A Martian enigma. (Copyright NASA.)

"So when the first overhead images of the Face became available, the presence of a seemingly well-preserved 'eye' became apparent vindication for proponents of artificiality on Mars. After all, it had been predicted by a testable hypothesis. Other 'secondary' features were noted as well: lip-like structures that defined a broad parted 'mouth,' 'nostrils' and others" (Ibid.).

Tonnies added that although none of these features offered definitive proof that the Face was the work of an extra-terrestrial intelligence, they did suggest the possibility that the Face, and perhaps other anomalies in its immediate vicinity, were far more than the mere tricks of light as claimed by NASA's public relations personnel. And if the Face *was* constructed by intelligent alien entities, rather than carved by the rigors of the Martian weather and the power of nature, then who were those same entities? Here's where we get into decidedly choppy waters, as we seek out the links between the Face on Mars and a certain other famous face. This one, however, is not found on Mars, but in the old sands of Egypt.

THE PYRAMIDS OF MARS

An Earth-Mars Connection

Most interpretations of the photographs of the Face on Mars that have been offered by both NASA and by certain elements of the mainstream scientific community suggest the Face is nothing more than an entirely natural landform that just happens to *look* like a Face. But, far more intriguing is the theory that the Face might very well represent the ruined remains of an ancient, artificial Sphinx-style monument of some kind, possibly one that was built by an indigenous, but now very long extinct, Martian civilization. In 1987, Mars anomaly researcher Richard Hoagland took things a large step further, and interpreted other nearby surface features as the remnants of a ruined city and possibly even artificially constructed pyramids, somewhat similar in appearance and nature to those of the ancient Egyptians of our very own world that still stand to this very day.

Mac Tonnies made an important statement that is directly relevant to this issue: "There is a superficial similarity between some of the alleged pyramids in the vicinity of the Face and the better-known ones here on Earth, such as the Egyptian pyramids and the Sphinx. This has become the stuff of endless arcane theorizing, and I agree with esoteric researchers that some sort of link between intelligence on Mars and Earth deserves to be taken seriously. But the formations on Mars are much, much larger than terrestrial architecture. This suggests a significantly different purpose, assuming they're intelligently designed" (Redfern, 2006).

The Secrets of the Sphinx

Like the somewhat-similar-looking structure at Cydonia, Mars, the Great Sphinx of Giza is located on the Giza Plateau on the Nile's west bank, is attention-grabbing, and is steeped in mystery. And although certainly not on the physical scale of the Face on Mars, the dimensions of the Sphinx are still most definitely impressive. More than 240 feet long, 20 feet wide, and in excess of 65 feet in height, the Sphinx faithfully holds court over all it dutifully surveys, both ancient and modern. As for its origins, well, this is where matters become confusing. The accepted position of Egyptology is that the Sphinx was constructed at some point between 2558 and 2532 BC, which was during the reign of the Pharaoh Khafre.

There are, however, problems with this scenario. And those problems suggest two things: (a) that the Sphinx was *not* constructed during the reign of Khafre, which was during the Fourth Dynasty; and (b) the Sphinx may possibly date long before Egyptian society was even fully established. It may, therefore, be much more correct to say that the Sphinx was *inherited* by the Egyptians, rather than having been *constructed* by them.

As for the issue of whether or not the Pharaoh Khafre was behind the creation of the Sphinx, late Egyptologist Selim Hassan made a highly valid point that casts some doubt on this scenario for a number of researchers. Hassan himself *was* inclined to accept that the Sphinx was probably made while Khafre ruled, but admitted that "there is not one single contemporary inscription which connects the Sphinx with Khafre; so, sound as it may appear, we must treat the evidence as circumstantial, until such time as a lucky turn of the spade of the excavator will reveal to the world a definite reference to the erection of the Sphinx" (Hassan, 1949).

The Great Sphinx of Egypt.
(Copyright Henry Bechard, 1880)

Eroding the Evidence

At the forefront of those who adhere to such beliefs is a geologist named Robert M. Schoch, PhD, an associate professor of natural dcience at the College of General Studies, Boston University. Much of Schoch's research has been focused on the theory that the Sphinx has been weathered and eroded by water at some point in its distant past—and, more importantly, by what appears to be rain water, and lots of it, too. But here's the challenging problem: The area in which the Sphinx sits has had an annual rainfall level of only around 1 inch since at least the days of Egypt's Old Kingdom (2686–2134 BC). And extensive rainfall seems to have gone right out of the window in Egypt during the third or fourth millennium BC. Thus, in Schoch's view, the Sphinx simply has to be much older than the world of Egyptology presently concludes it to be. Incredibly, Schoch suspects the age of the Sphinx may be in the region of 7,000 years, and perhaps even more than that.

To Egyptologists, this is complete and utterly outrageous anathema. Many have tried to explain away the puzzle of the weathering of the Sphinx in a fashion that allows for it to have been constructed in more recent times. Robert Temple who was watched closely by the CIA and British Intelligence following the publication of his 1976 book, *The Sirius Mystery,* theorized that perhaps the Sphinx was once surrounded by a moat. Maybe, therefore, it was moat water, rather than rain water, that led to the noticeable erosion? Schoch is not persuaded by this scenario. He notes that "the bedrock in the enclosure is highly faulted" and would certainly have "leaked like a sieve" (Schoch, 2011).

Climatologists Rudolph Kuper and Stefan Kröpelin, of the University of Cologne, and Judith Bunbury, a geologist at St. Edmund's College, Cambridge, England, have voiced their opinions that the period in which Egypt was transformed from a land where rainfall was fairly significant, to the more familiar state of harsh, hot dryness that dominates the Giza Plateau today, may actually have been much later than many have concluded. If true, this would have allowed for the creation of the Sphinx during the time frame widely accepted by most Egyptologists, and all would be well.

Schoch has made a very logical rebuttal to this theory: There are other structures in the vicinity of the Sphinx that do *not* show evidence of water-based weathering, but those structures *do* date from the time periods in which Egyptologists accept the Sphinx, was created. If those other structures do not show evidence of such weathering, why does the Sphinx if it was built in the very same era? In Schoch's view, the answer is as clear and simple as it is controversy-fueled and filled: The Sphinx obviously *wasn't* constructed during that same time frame.

Inheriting the Sphinx

Robert Schoch has also stated his belief that rather than being the brains behind the Sphinx, the Pharaoh Khafre remodeled it according to his own design. On this point, Schoch makes the important observation that, at some point long, long ago, significant changes appear to have been made to the head of Sphinx. It is, without doubt, far too small when compared to its body. Schoch says that, in its original form, the head would have been weathered in much the same way as the body appears to have been. He believes it was re-carved, in dynastic periods, and during the process the head was reduced in size. Schoch has also considered the possibility that rather than looking very human, as it certainly does today, in its original form—prior to Khafre's transformation—the Sphinx may have represented the form of the lion. Interestingly, Richard Hoagland has argued that the Face on Mars seems to possess feline qualities, too.

Pharaohs on Mars

The Face on Mars/Egyptian Sphinx controversy aside, let us take a careful look at additional data that might be suggestive of a link between the huge structures of Egypt and the even larger ones of Mars. Aside from the Face itself, certainly the most important player in this entire saga is what has become known as the D&M Pyramid, so named after the computer imaging specialists who discovered it: Vincent DiPietro and Gregory Molenaar. A five-sided structure, also situated in Cydonia, the D&M Pyramid is not in particularly good condition. Visibly cracked, pummeled, and even seemingly melted in part, it appears to have been subjected to an internal explosion. An explosion provoked by who, or what, remains unknown.

Still on the matter of the D&M Pyramid, the *Enterprise Mission* Website noted that the bottom, triangular facet of the pyramid is bracketed by what appears to be a pair of rectilinear formations that could have been constructed to act as buttresses. In addition, on that same facet, said Mac Tonnies, can be seen a shallow crack "identical to the ruined brick casing seen on the Pyramids of Egypt." Tonnies concluded this strongly represented "a protective veneer of some sort." This is something paralleled by the Great Pyramid at Giza, which on its completion was covered by a veneer of polished white limestone. Today, most of the limestone is unfortunately gone, but in mightier and earlier times, it must surely have made for a spectacular sight when the Sun was reflected upon the stone, turning the pyramid into a huge, glowing beacon in the deserts of Egypt (Tonnies, 2004).

Moving on from the D&M Pyramid, Cydonia is home to a *second* five-sided creation: It is known in Face on Mars research circles as the City Pyramid. Truly, this is a structure of immense proportions, easily eclipsing anything that surfaced out of Egypt, and into which the Great Pyramid could easily fit. Granted, it was speculation on his part, but Tonnies wondered if the City Pyramid might have acted as a huge shield for some form of city-like environment, perhaps one designed to try to protect at least a percentage of the Martian population when they realized the atmosphere and eco-system of their precious world was beginning to irreversibly degrade and collapse all around them.

That there appears to be yet *another* huge formation on the surface of Mars that looks very Egyptian in nature has led some commentators to address the highly controversial theory that it represents the profile view of none other than the Egyptian Queen Nefertiti, whom Jeane Dixon wrote about, and the CIA took secret notice of Dixon's work in the 1960s. Whether pareidolia or not, Mac Tonnies could not deny the Egyptian connection, and added that, whatever the Nefertiti-like formation represented, it had been "deposited in a striking feminine likeness" (Ibid).

Should the Egyptian-like formations at Cydonia one day be proved artificial, then the immensely huge question is, surely, who built them? Do they represent the work of home-grown Martians, or perhaps some visiting ancient civilization that originated from far outside of our solar system? Mac Tonnies had his own particular theories and ideas on this issue: "It's possible that the complex in Cydonia, as well as potential edifices elsewhere on Mars, were constructed by indigenous Martians. Mars was once extremely Earth-like. We know it had liquid water. It's perfectly conceivable that a civilization arose on Mars and managed to build structures that are within our ability to investigate. Or, the anomalies might be evidence of interstellar visitation: Perhaps the remains of a colony of some sort" (Redfern, 2006).

Disaster Strikes

If Mars *was* once home to intelligent life, and if NASA really *has* stumbled upon evidence—hard or suggestive—of that very same intelligence, in the form of the enigmatic Face, then how was an apparently once-thriving planet transformed into the utterly dead and dusty—or *presumed* dead and dusty—world that we see today? And how did its civilization meet its end? Mac Tonnies had some intriguing ideas with respect to these particular questions: "Astronomer Tom Van Flandern has proposed that Mars was once the moon of a tenth planet that literally exploded in the distant past. If so, then the explosion would have had severe effects on Mars, probably rendering it uninhabitable. That's one rather apocalyptic scenario. Another is that Mars's atmosphere was destroyed by the impact that produced the immense Hellas Basin. Both ideas are fairly heretical by current standards. Mainstream planetary science is much more comfortable with Mars dying a slow, prolonged death. Pyrotechnic collisions simply aren't intellectually fashionable, despite evidence that such things are much more commonplace than we'd prefer" (Ibid.).

But why, if a theoretical Martian empire was indeed destroyed countless thousands of years ago, should its architecture have apparently looked so Egyptian-like? Let's now turn our attention to the most amazing of all possibilities.

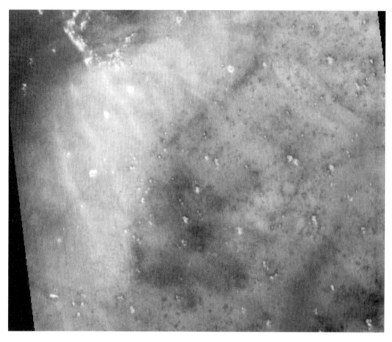

Found on Mars: A Nefertiti-style design. (Copyright NASA.)

From Cydonia to Giza

Mac Tonnies was, undeniably, very careful and thoughtful when publicly addressing what he believed and didn't believe, what he saw as theory versus fact, and what he interpreted as speculation versus hard evidence. On this latter point, Tonnies speculated—and was the first to admit that speculation is precisely what it was—that if Mars did suffer from some planet-wide disaster in its distant past, as suggested by Tom Van Flandern, then maybe its inhabitants had a degree of forewarning that allowed at least some of them to flee the dark apocalypse that was closing in, day by day.

Perhaps, Tonnies suggested, when the final countdown was upon them, the panicked Martians quickly launched an armada of spacecraft in the direction of Earth, hoping and praying to find some way of preventing the total obliteration of their race. Maybe, against all the odds and the perils inherent in dicey interplanetary spaceflight, they landed relatively successfully, and then began the long and laborious process of starting over in those areas of our planet where civilization and evidence of astonishing building techniques and advanced technologies appeared to spring up out of nowhere. This would, of course, include Central America, South America, the Middle East, and India. And, Tonnies hypothesized, perhaps those Martian survivors, wishing to see at least some part of their obliterated Martian society, culture, and heritage live on for generations to come, taught and encouraged the primitive humans they encountered to embrace, and elaborate on, the original Martian penchant for pyramids, sphinxes, and other gigantic, stone-based formations.

Was this just a theory on the part of Tonnies? Yes, it was. But, sometimes, theories also turn out to be the truth. Maybe, one day, Tonnies's musings on this aspect of the Face on Mars issue will be seen as much more. Possibly, those musings will be utterly vindicated and we'll have a solid answer as to why, from the Face on Mars to the D&M Pyramid, and from the Nefertiti-type image to the City Pyramid, Egypt and the Red Planet seem to be so inextricably, and mysteriously, tied together.

Modern-Day Martians

Even if a number of Martians did survive some Armageddon-type event by fleeing to our world, perhaps the calamity that overtook Mars did not erase everything that lived and breathed on or under its surface. On this subject, Mac Tonnies reported that: "The Mars Global Surveyor has taken images of anomalous, branching objects that look like organic phenomena. [The late science-fiction author] Arthur C. Clarke, for one, was sold on the prospect of large forms of life on Mars, and had been highly critical of JPL's [the Jet Propulsion Laboratory's] silence. Clarke's most impressive candidates are what he termed 'Banyan Trees' seen near Mars' south pole. And he collaborated with Mars researcher Greg Orme in a study of similar features that NASA has termed 'black spiders;' root like formations that suggest tenacious, macroscopic life. And: Mars has water. It's been found underground, frozen. If we melted all of it we'd have an ankle-deep ocean enveloping the entire planet. I predict we will find more of it" (Ibid.).

A Time Before Ours

Mac Tonnies had another alternative theory, too, for the Face on Mars—one that had nothing to do with Martians. But one that had everything to do with us, the human race. He wondered if we and the Martians were one and the same. Echoing the stories about fantastic, nuclear-armed flying craft, Vimanas, soaring around the skies of India during the ancient time frame described within the *Mahabharata*, Tonnies pondered the astounding possibility that perhaps, in the deep and distant past, a long-gone and equally long-forgotten race of people from our very own

Earth achieved space flight, traveled to Mars, and created the immense creations that many, today, suggest were the work of Martians:

"In retrospect," said Tonnies, "I regret not spending more time in [my] book [*After the Martian Apocalypse*] addressing the possibility that the Face was built by a vanished terrestrial civilization that had achieved space flight. That was a tough notion to swallow, even as speculation, as it raises as many [new] questions as it answers" (Redfern, 2004).

It certainly *is* a tough notion to swallow. But, it might go some significant way toward explaining why certain structures at Cydonia and Egypt seem to extend beyond mere superficial similarity. It was a theory that Tonnies followed up on in *The Cryptoterrestrials*, published posthumously in early 2010. And it's a theory that derives some support from former Special Agent Walter Bosley of the U.S. Air Force Office of Special Investigations.

Ancient Humanoids

Walter Bosley's father served in the U.S. Air Force in the late 1950s, on matters relative to the U.S. space program. Significantly, during the period of his employment with the military, Bosley's father received at Wright-Patterson Air Force Base, Ohio, a classified briefing relative to the reported legendary UFO crash at Roswell, New Mexico, in the summer of 1947. Bosley said that by the time of his father's briefing, the U.S. Air Force had come to a startling conclusion: Neither the strange aerial device nor the bodies found in the desert outside of Roswell at the time in question had alien origins.

Very significantly, Bosley revealed, his father told him the entities and their craft came from *inside* our planet. They were among the survivors of a very ancient civilization that ruled our planet thousands of years ago, supposedly residing within a huge, underground system of caverns and tunnels beneath the southwest portion of the United States. Bosley was additionally told by his father, "They are human in appearance, so much so that they can move among us with ease with just a little effort. If you get a close look, you'd notice something odd, but not if the person just passed you on the street." Bosley's father was not the only one to comment on matters relative to an ancient terrestrial race that had developed advanced technologies and which was manifested in spectacular style (Guest, 2005).

Cayce and the Sphinx

Born in 1877, Edgar Cayce was, without doubt, one of the United States's most famous of all psychics. He still retains a massive and faithful following, long after his death in 1945 at the age of 67. H.P. Albarelli, Jr., who worked in the White House of President Jimmy Carter, and for the U.S. Department of Treasury, has stated that at some point during the early 1960s researchers of the CIA's Technical Services Staff who were at the forefront of mind-altering research were particularly interested in the work of Cayce. Albarelli has revealed that certain consultants acted undercover at the Association for Research and Enlightenment, which was contained within Cayce's Virginia Beach–based headquarters. Clearly, then, someone in the CIA was following the stories of Cayce, which seem to have been born out of research closely paralleling that of Andrija Puharich.

In the 1960s, the CIA secretly infiltrated the Edgar Cayce Foundation. (Copyright Nick Redfern.)

Certainly, one of Cayce's favorite pet subjects was that of the legendary land of Atlantis, and its equally legendary people—first referred to in the writings of Plato around 360 BC. According to Cayce's beliefs, in the very distant past, a series of catastrophic events, including one akin to a land-engulfing biblical flood, irreversibly decimated the Atlantean society, wherever it might have been situated. And, lord knows, numerous parts of the world have been suggested as viable candidates, including the Atlantic Ocean, the Mediterranean, the Canary Islands, the Azores, and many more. But, regardless of the location of Atlantis, Cayce was sure of the outcome of the disaster: The survivors were forced to start over anew, in parts foreign and exotic. One of those locations, maintained Cayce, was Egypt. Thus, in Cayce's mind, it was the Atlanteans who brought the astonishing technology to early Egypt that eventually allowed for the creation of the Sphinx and the pyramids.

How did Cayce know this? He claimed, admittedly very controversially, to have been the reincarnation of an Egyptian priest named Ra Ta, supposedly the creator of a healing center in Egypt known as the Temple of Sacrifice. Cayce also stated that his past-life knowledge of Egypt included his awareness of a fantastic hall of records located underneath the right-paw of the Sphinx. Those priceless records, Cayce maintained, told the true and unexpurgated history of Atlantis, its people, and its ultimate destruction thousands of years in the dim and distant past.

Incredibly, while carefully studying the Sphinx in person, Robert Schoch reported that he and his team had "discovered clear evidence of a cavity or chamber under the left paw of the Sphinx. For what it is worth, some have suggested to me that this may be a 'Hall of Records.'" At the time, said Schoch, he was not aware of Edgar Cayce's similar predictions (Schoch, 2011).

Perhaps, one day, the sub-surface secrets of the Sphinx's paw(s) will finally surface, and perhaps Edgar Cayce will be vindicated. And maybe, in view of the enlightening revelations of H.P. Albarelli, Jr., about Cayce, the CIA has its very own Hall of Records on *all* of the noteworthy topics dissected in this chapter. If so, perhaps in our search for answers about the Face on Mars and its many attendant puzzles, we should stop looking skyward and start looking into the secret vaults of officialdom. In fact, that's exactly what we're going to do right now.

MARTIAN
CONSPIRACIES

It will surely surprise no one to learn that the Face on Mars has become the champion of conspiracy theorists just about everywhere. Many would say with very good reason, too. Chiefly, there are three key ingredients to the cosmic conspiracy: (a) NASA is actively hiding its knowledge that the Face on Mars is artificial and is somehow connected to the pyramids of Egypt; (b) elements of NASA and the U.S. government have known about the existence of the Face for far longer than most of us assume or realize; and (c) in the 1950s attempts may have been officially initiated, but that were ultimately aborted by the start of the 1960s, to subtly inform the populace of its existence, nature, and origin. Let's look at the evidence for those three allegations of conspiracy.

We'll start with a two-pronged attack, one that suggests someone has known about the Face on Mars for far longer than most of us anticipate, and that attempts were made, decades ago, to get the story behind the Face into the public domain.

Although conspiracy theorists have been unable to prove how and why certain people within the U.S. government may have known of the existence of the Face on Mars long before its 1976 discovery by *Viking 1*, there are a couple of notable issues that *could* be used to support the notion that (a) the Face and the attendant pyramid-type structures in its immediate vicinity were known of as far back as the 1950s; and (b) the popular media of the day may have been used by the government to slowly and carefully present such data to the public, and prepare them for the time when the full story would finally be revealed.

The Space Cadet

Tom Corbett, Space Cadet was a 1950s-era science fiction phenomenon that had its origins in Robert Heinlein's 1948 novel *Space Cadet* and Joseph Greene's *Tom Ranger and the Space Cadets* series of broadly the same time frame. Novels, comic books, daily and Sunday newspaper strips, and even a television series were spawned as a result of the huge interest in the *Space Cadet* adventures of the 1950s. Then there is a 3-D View-Master version of the *Tom Corbett* tales. And it's here that we take careful steps into the conspiracy zone.

Twenty-one three-dimensional Kodachrome pictures comprise the trio of reels that go by the title of *The Moon Pyramid*, *The Red Planet*, and *The Mystery of the Asteroid*. They start with the tale of a futuristic astronaut assigned to a mining project in the heart of the Asteroid Belt. While at work on one particular asteroid, the miner stumbles upon what looks like some sort of archaeological relic. Pyramid-like in shape, and coated in hieroglyphics that resemble the work of the Egyptians, an ancient artifact is exactly what has been found. Speculation abounds that the Asteroid Belt is the remains of a world home to intelligent aliens that once existed between Mars and Jupiter, a theory not at all unlike the exploding planet theory of Tom Van Flandern, as noted by Mac Tonnies.

From the dark depths of the Asteroid Belt, the *Tom Corbett* story then takes us to our very own Moon, where a similar pyramid-type structure has been found. But it's more than just that. When placed together, the two creations comprise a singular object that allows for a holographic viewing of Mars and that reveals some astounding imagery on the surface of the Red Planet. Anxious to capitalize on this astounding discovery, a team of astronauts heads to Mars, where they find nothing less than a massive, 1,000-foot-high pyramid, a number of obelisks, and even a small, carved face displaying feline attributes. A closer comparison to what was uncovered by Face on Mars researchers, decades later, one would be extremely hard-pressed to ever find.

It is this very curious set of coincidences (or, for those who see things a very different way, a set of deliberate actions) that has ignited controversial speculation suggesting the feline face and the pyramid structures found on NASA photographs in the 1970s were secretly known to the U.S. government way back in the 1950s, and that maybe someone on the inside was determined to subtly let the rest of us know about this cosmic discovery, possibly even with a degree of official sanction.

These strange circumstances and theories are made all the more intriguing by the fact that a certain figure hired as a consultant to the *Tom Corbett* franchise had links to the secret world of government and military. His name was Willy Ley, a German rocket genius whose published work, and particularly his 1957 book, *Rockets, Missiles, and Space Travel*, played an officially recognized role in dictating the U.S. government's policies regarding space exploration. Ley also inspired much of the work of Werner von Braun, a German expert in rocketry, who, after working for Hitler during World War II, came to the United States via a top-secret program called *Paperclip*. Von Braun ultimately rose to the rank of director of NASA. Willy Ley, then, moved in interesting and powerful circles.

Another person who wrote about a pyramid link to Mars was author Otto Binder, who, using the pseudonym Eando Binder, penned a science fiction novel in 1971 called *Puzzle of the Space Pyramids*, which also dealt with a discovery by the human race of ancient pyramids on Mars. In Binder's novel, the pyramids act as gravity generators designed to manipulate time and space. Binder was also a believer in UFOs, and wrote a number of non-fiction books on the subject. Interestingly, his 1976 book co-written with Max Flindt, *Mankind: Child of the Stars*, included a foreword from Erich Von Daniken. Even more interesting: In Binder's *Victory in Space* book, the foreword was supplied by *Tom Corbett* consultant Willy Ley. Otto Binder, too, it seems, kept intriguing company.

Mars: a world of puzzles. (Copyright NASA.)

The Face of Jack Kirby

In 1958, Harvey Comics published a three-part comic book series under the collective banner of *Race for the Moon*. Both penned and illustrated by comic-book legend Jack Kirby of Marvel Comics fame, and co-creator with Stan Lee of the *Fantastic Four*, the *Incredible Hulk*, the *Avengers*, and numerous other superhero characters, it is issue two of the series, titled *The Face on Mars*, that needs our attention.

In Kirby's story, an American astronaut named Ben Fisher leads a team to Mars, where, dominating the Martian landscape, they are astounded to find a gigantic human face carved out of rock.

The adventurous Fisher elects to climb the huge face, and in doing so finds to his surprise that the eyes of the immense creation are actually cave-like entrance points to a vast kingdom hidden deep inside the face itself. While investigating the old, long-abandoned structure, Fisher has a vision in which he sees ancient Martians doing battle with hostile aliens whose home world, interestingly, was a planet whose ultimate destruction by the Martians led to the creation of the Asteroid Belt. And here's the kicker: Jack Kirby had secret associations with officialdom—in fact, with none other than the CIA.

The Agency and the Artist

In the late 1970s, a screenwriter named Barry Ira Geller obtained the movie rights to a science fiction novel written in 1968 by Roger Zelazny. Its title was *Lord of Light*. By November 1979, the movie option was much more than that. Ambitious planning was in the works to turn Zelazny's story—which tells of the crew of a spacecraft called the *Star of India*, who crash on a faraway world and are forced to begin life anew—into a multimillion-dollar movie. As part of his plans to bring the movie to fruition, Geller sought out Jack Kirby to prepare artwork that would hopefully capture the spirit and theme of *Lord of Light* and also help in the efforts to find funding to bring the story to life on the cinematic screen. Kirby's drawings on his very own ancient astronauts-themed comic book series of the mid-1970s, *The Eternals*, displayed precisely the sort of thing that Geller was looking for. But, despite the initial optimism that surrounded the project, due to legal problems, the movie was eventually shelved. It was, however, briefly resurrected by none other than agents of the CIA, who were particularly enamored of both the story and Jack Kirby's art—for reasons truly bizarre.

In 1979, when the country of Iran descended into chaos and internal strife, a number of American hostages were held at the American Embassy in the nation's capital of Tehran. Of those, six employees of the U.S. Department of State succeeded in evading their Iranian captors and managed to make a run for it. They found a safe haven in the Canadian Embassy, where they remained for approximately 12 weeks. But: How to get them home without the Iranians realizing who they were when they tried to board a plane out of Iran? It was then, with this particularly troubling question in mind, that the CIA came up with a brain-wave.

The plan was to have the six pose as members of a Canadian movie-making company who were in Iran to make an on-screen version of *Lord of Light*. Then, with faked Canadian passports made by the CIA's finest, and make-up and wigs provided by special effects expert John Chambers, who worked on the 1968 movie *Planet of the Apes*, the plotline was to have the group leave Iran and, if questioned at the airport by security officials, say they were heading back home to Canada now that the filming of *Lord of Light* was over.

Antonio J. Mendez was the man behind the CIA mission. Years later, he came clean and said: "Because *Star Wars* had made it big only recently, many science fiction, fantasy, and superhero films were being produced. We decided we needed a script with 'sci-fi,' Middle Eastern, and mythological elements. Something about the glory of Islam would be nice, too" (Mendez, 1999-2000).

Mendez said that it was John Chambers who suggested *Lord of Light* would be the ideal candidate—and history has shown that it most certainly was. Carrying copies of Jack Kirby's original artwork (and also a significant body of *new* artwork that the CIA had secretly requested Kirby create specifically for the operation) to help support the story that they were in Iran to make a movie, the six had no trouble clearing security at the airport, and boarded a 5:30 a.m. flight first to Zurich, Switzerland, and then a second one, which was United States–bound.

Jack Kirby's connections to the CIA were far from over, however.

Also in the late 1970s, CIA personnel quietly asked Kirby to provide them with his own artistic designs and thoughts relative to (a) a jet-pack-type device that would allow agency personnel and troops to fly into the battlefield in a fashion most famously portrayed by Sean Connery's James Bond, 007 in the 1965 movie *Thunderball*; and (b) a vast undersea military installation of a type that would surely have befitted a power-crazed villain of the aforementioned James Bond.

Swift's Secrets

The scenario that people in government, who, years prior to NASA's release of its Face on Mars imagery, possessed classified knowledge of the nature of Mars is certainly controversial. But there are other examples where matters of a Martian nature were apparently anticipated long before they were confirmed and that also spill over into the realm of official secrecy.

The Martian moon, Phobos. (Copyright NASA.)

In 1726 Benjamin Motte, of England, published one of the most well-known of all fantasy novels: *Gulliver's Travels*, written by Jonathan Swift. While on the island of Laputa, Gulliver learns that the nation's scientists have "discovered two lesser stars, or satellites, which revolve about Mars; whereof the innermost is distant from the center of the primary planet exactly three of its diameters, and the outermost five; the former revolves in the space of ten hours, and the latter in twenty one and a half; so that the squares of their periodical times are very near in the same proportion with the cubes of their distance from the center of Mars; which evidently shows them to be governed by the same law of gravitation that influences the other heavenly bodies" (Swift, 1996).

Mars certainly does have two moons: Phobos and Deimos. When Swift's novel was first published, in 1726, however, no one had any inkling at all that Mars possessed a pair of orbiting satellites. They were not even discovered until 1877, more than 150 years after *Gulliver's Travels* was published. Of course, it could have all been down to chance and coincidence. But, if it was, Swift was not too far off when it came to his in-print descriptions of Phobos and Deimos.

The former is located around 3,728 miles from Mars, and circles the planet in just more than seven-and-a-half hours. In *Gulliver's Travels*, Swift provided his readers with the figures of 8,077 miles and 10 hours. Deimos averages 12,490 miles from the Red Planet and it orbits the planet in a little more than 30 hours. In his book, Swift gave statistics of 16,900 and 21.5 hours. Although these figures are not right on target, they are not a million miles off target either. So, how did Swift uncover the fact that Mars has two moons, a century and a half before they were even officially discovered?

The World's Most Mysterious Manuscript

A former U.S. Intelligence employee named Robert Manners maintains that Swift secured his information from at least partially deciphering certain sections of none other than the controversial Voynich Manuscript, which, he says, is of ongoing interest to the Pentagon. A mysterious,

240-page, early-15th-century document written totally in cipher, or in some wholly unknown language, by an equally unknown author, the Voynich Manuscript is named after a book-dealer of Polish-Lithuanian descent, Wilfrid Voynich, who purchased it in 1912. It contains illustrations of both a botanical and biological nature, and also includes 26 intriguing images of astronomical and astrological phenomena relative to our sun, our Moon, the planets, and the stars. Manners may be proved correct about U.S. Intelligence's interest in the story of the Voynich Manuscript and its relationship to Jonathan Swift.

The National Security Agency has released into the public domain a number of papers written about the Voynich Manuscript by NSA-connected figures who were trying valiantly to decipher its contents. They include James R. Child's *The Voynich Manuscript Revisited*, in which the author hypothesized that the manuscript was written in a Northern Germanic dialect. Brigadier John H. Tiltman's Voynich-themed *The Most Mysterious Manuscript in the World* is a paper that the NSA has also now made available to the public. Tiltman was a British citizen and an expert code-breaker, who spent many years working for the British equivalent of the National Security Agency, the Government Communications Headquarters (GCHQ), before acting in a consultancy capacity for the NSA between 1964 and 1980. Tiltman also had the distinction of being the first non-American to be recognized as a member of the NSA's prestigious Hall of Honor.

When asked how, and under what particular circumstances, he secured the extraordinary data suggesting Jonathan Swift deciphered at least parts of the Voynich Manuscript and, on doing so, had learned something important about the Martian Moons, Robert Manners stated that the papers on the Voynich Manuscript the NSA has declassified only represent a small portion of a far bigger collection that, he believes, will only surface when, and if, the NSA chooses to reveal more from its secret archives.

NASA is fully aware of the curious affair of Jonathan Swift and his early anticipation that Mars has two moons, but prefers to suggest a far more down-to-earth explanation for the controversy: "Long before their discovery in 1877, Johannes Kepler [a German mathematician and astronomer] speculated that since the Earth had one moon and Jupiter had four known in his time, Mars might have two moons since it orbits between Earth and Jupiter" (Dick, 2007).

NASA concludes that Swift may have been influenced by Kepler's theory, which is known as Celestial Harmony. And it cannot be entirely discounted as having played a role in determining certain aspects of the writings of Jonathan Swift. Unfortunately, however, no one—not even the finest minds of NASA—has ever been able to provide an absolutely 100-percent-satisfactory answer as to how Swift predicted, with an admittedly fair degree of accuracy for the time period in question, the number of moons that orbit Mars, their sizes, and their distances from the planet itself.

Perhaps, after all, it really was a matter of chance, coincidence, synchronicity, or Swift's personal acceptance of Johannes Kepler's Celestial Harmony. But whatever the real answer to this centuries-old puzzle, just like Jack Kirby and the brains behind the *Tom Corbett, Space Cadet* stories, Jonathan Swift brought to the table a Martian controversy that was incredibly ahead of its time. And, now, onto the third part of the conspiracy: That officialdom, since the dawning of the 1960s, has chosen to *hide* the truth of the Face on Mars, rather than subtly promote it, as may well have been briefly attempted by some faction of the U.S. government in the 1950s.

An argument most certainly *can* be made that the sagas of *Tom Corbett, Space Cadet* and Jack Kirby's *The Face on Mars* were part of an effort designed to get people thinking about the idea of a carved, ancient, alien face on the surface of Mars and, in relation to *Tom Corbett*, one that also had a pyramid connection. But what of the notion that maybe that situation has changed drastically, and there is now a desire to dumb us all down and keep us in the dark on the case for the Face?

On the issue of a government conspiracy to hide information relative to the Face on Mars, Mac Tonnies noted that when NASA's Jet Propulsion Laboratory released the first Mars Global Surveyor image of the Face in 1998, "they chose to subject the image to a high-pass filter that made the Face look hopelessly vague. This was almost certainly done as a deliberate attempt to nullify public interest in a feature that the space agency is determined to ignore. So yes, there is a cover-up, of sorts. But it's in plain view for anyone who cares to look into the matter objectively. I could speculate endlessly on the forms a more nefarious cover-up might take; but the fact remains that the Surveyor continues to return high-resolution images" (Redfern, 2004).

Tonnies added on this matter: "Speculation and even some healthy paranoia are useful tools. But we need to stay within the bounds of verifiable fact, lest we become the very conspiracy-mongering caricatures painted by the mainstream media" (Ibid.).

Maybe we do have verifiable fact that has a bearing on the approach the U.S. government and NASA have taken with respect to the Face on Mars.

The Brookings Artifacts

As the 1960s began, and as NASA's programs to further explore outer space grew, the Brookings Institution (a "think tank" dedicated to contract studies on areas such as economy and foreign policy) prepared an extensive and illuminating paper for NASA's Committee on Long Range Studies. Its overall title was *Proposed Studies on the Implications of Peaceful Space Activities for Human Affairs*, and it delved deeply into NASA's future role in space, what the agency might expect to find once it began exploring realms far beyond our own, and future trends in space travel. Brookings also offered thought-provoking opinions on the issue of alien life.

Very interestingly, it was hypothesized within the pages of the document that perhaps ancient objects, devices, or structures created by intelligent aliens might one day be found on the surface of the Moon or even on the surface of some of the nearby planets in our solar system (Mars, maybe?). The Brookings Report also suggested such discoveries of an ancient structure nature might one day provide NASA with clues, and maybe even hard evidence, suggesting strongly that life out there had, at some point in our long and turbulent history, been far closer to home than we might ever have previously considered even remotely possible.

Most intriguing of all, the Brookings document did not only discuss the possibility of finding alien artifacts or structures on nearby worlds; it also addressed the matter of *if*—rather than *when*—the general public should be informed of any such discoveries. And, if that were not enough, NASA was warned by Brookings of how a revelation to the public that alien artifacts had been found might result in the disintegration of our whole society and civilization when faced with highly advanced extra-terrestrial civilizations whose cultures, beliefs, and ideologies were very different from ours. The consequences of such discoveries and revelations, said Brookings, in clear, deliberate, and grave warning tones to NASA, were wildly unpredictable.

Mac Tonnies noted an important factor in relation to this controversial document: "If our own history is any example, technologically robust civilizations inevitably subsume less sophisticated cultures, not merely by violently dismantling them, but by introducing a virulent strain of apathy. The infamous Brookings report to NASA, recommending that the discovery of extraterrestrial artifacts be covered up for fear of paralyzing research and development enterprises, stands as perhaps the most explicit elucidation of this idea" (Redfern, 2006).

Clearly, if the *Tom Corbett*/Jack Kirby affairs of the 1950s *were* attempts on the part of some insider sources to get the message out about the Face on Mars, it appears that by the time the Brookings Report came on the scene at the start of the 1960s, there had been a distinct about-turn. Silence was the order of the day, recommended Brookings. And NASA, it seems, duly agreed. But, why should the discovery of life on Mars—perhaps even life that was somehow linked in ways not fully understood with the people of ancient Egypt and elsewhere on our world—be an issue deemed vital of being withheld from us? Mac Tonnies had a theory that may not have been too far off the mark, should we one day learn the incredible truth. Of the appearance of the Face on Mars, Tonnies asked a simple, yet vitally important, question: "Why a humanoid face?" (Redfern, 2004).

In answer to his important question about why the Face on Mars looks so uncannily human-like in appearance, Tonnies eloquently worded it in a fashion that may very well get right to the thumping heart of the government's deepest and darkest suspicions about our mysterious past: "That's the disquieting aspect of the whole inquiry. It suggests that the human race has something to do with Mars, that our history is woefully incomplete, that our understanding of biology and evolution might be in store for a violent upheaval" (Ibid.).

The Face on Mars is millions of miles away from us, it might have been created near-countless millennia ago, and its long-gone sculptors—Martians or ancient, advanced humans—are now solidly absorbed into our culture, legends, and folklore; their real identities lost, forgotten, obscured, and mutated. But, for as long as it stares upward from the Martian surface, practically calling for—even *demanding*—our attention, the Face on Mars will likely be an enigma both vexing and troubling to those power-wielders on our planet whose only goal is to maintain, and control, the status quo.

Violent upheaval, as Mac Tonnies worded it, and of the very type that the Face on Mars has the real potential to create, is the absolute last thing our leaders want.

THE CIRCLES
OF DOOMSDAY

Each and every summer, stretching back decades, the British landscape has been targeted by someone's, or something's, amazing artwork of the landscape variety. I'm talking, of course, about crop circles. Crop circles are without any doubt one of the biggest and most captivating mysteries of the modern era. Numerous theories have been advanced to try and explain the phenomenon; opinions, however, remain sharply divided.

For some, crop circles are the work of benign extra-terrestrials. Others see the spirit of the Earth itself, pleading to the people of the planet to change their destructive and violent ways, as being wholly responsible. Then there is the notion that all of the crop circles have man-made origins, or that they are possibly the results of sophisticated and covert military weapons testing. Whatever the ultimate truth of the matter, the phenomenon is one that shows no signs of disappearing anytime soon. It's also a phenomenon that has attracted the attention of the National Security Agency (NSA) for reasons that stretch back to the era of our old friends the Mayans. But, before we get to the NSA, a bit of background evidence on the way in which officialdom began its study of this puzzle that, at times literally, has had its personnel secretly going around in circles.

Wartime Circles

Under the terms of the British government's Freedom of Information legislation, a number of records concerning the wartime activities of Britain's Security Service, MI5, have been declassified and made available for inspection at the National Archive in London. Among the many files that tell fascinating stories of once-secret operations of the service, one from the height of World War II stands out in particular. The relevant file begins:

"The early days of 1940 and 1941 produced an avalanche of reports about the spies and fifth columnists who many people thought were roaming the land unhindered. Each village boasted of enemy agents in their midst, and it is only by recapturing the atmosphere of those days that one can see the matter in its proper perspective. Everyone had heard of the activities of fifth columnists on the continent and of the alarmingly successful part they had played in the overthrow of France and Belgium. It was therefore natural with everyone tense for the threatened invasion that so many reports came in. Each had to be investigated, even if only to put the minds of the public and the services at rest" (Security Service, 1946).

The report continues, and outlines the nature of its content: "This account is not concerned with the activities of fifth columnists such as sabotage, capturing airfields and key points, and harassing the defending army, but in the methods used in communicating to each other and to the enemy. Reports from Poland, Holland, France and Belgium showed that they used ground markings for the guidance of bombers and paratroops (and of lights by night). Such ground markings might be the cutting of cornfields into guiding marks for aircraft" (Ibid.).

On this intriguing matter, MI5 elaborated that, from interviews conducted with personnel who had taken part in the hostilities in Poland, it had been determined that one of the ways that Nazi spies might have been communicating with German Luftwaffe pilots was by "beating out signs, twenty meters in diameter, on harrowed fields or mowing such signs on meadows or cornfields" (Ibid.).

Notably, however, despite the widespread discovery of such formations, no definitive evidence ever surfaced to suggest that the strange creations found all across Europe in the early 1940s were the work of the Nazis. This was merely a theory to try to explain a tangible, real mystery and nothing more. The files also reveal that MI5 agents were secretly dispatched throughout the UK to examine similar crop formations found in British fields during the war, in an attempt to determine if they, too, were linked with the activities of the Nazis. And though the investigations did not confirm this hypothesis, the files are a perfect example and, more importantly, an *officially documented* example, of the fact that crop circles are not just a phenomenon of the modern era, but were reported to, and investigated by, high-level government departments 70 years ago. And it's still going on today.

The U.S. Government Takes Note

Agents of American officialdom were in attendance at the first European meeting of the *Society for Scientific Exploration*, which was held on August 7–8, 1992, in Munich, and that had the crop circle subject on its agenda. A three-page document pertaining to the conference, originally classified at secret level, has been made available under the terms of the Freedom of Information Act by the Defense Intelligence Agency. Its contents make for interesting reading:

"The expressed aim of the SSE meeting was to promote the exchange of ideas, results, and goals among researchers in various fields of anomalies, and inform the public of the discussion among active scientists concerning current controversial issues. Papers and communications were in English, and German language abstracts of the various parapsychology (PS) papers presented were distributed at the beginning of the meeting. The conference sessions examined PSI and other extraordinary mental phenomena, crop circles (were they messages or hoaxes), geophysical variables and their influences on human behavior, astro-psychology, the Earth and unidentified flying objects (UFO), and additional highlights, to include near death experiences (NDE)" (Defense Intelligence Agency, 1992).

But, far more substantial is what the National Security Agency has had to say on the crop circle issue.

Crop Circles and 2012

Established by President Harry S. Truman in 1952, and operating out of Fort Meade, Maryland, the NSA has the huge and daunting task of eavesdropping, on a massive scale, on potentially hostile nations—and occasionally, history has shown, on friendly nations and even on its very own citizens, too. The NSA is also mandated to crack codes and ciphers, analyze a wide variety of intelligence-themed data; monitor e-mails, telephone calls, and faxes; and generally keep its powerful, watchful eyes and ears on the world 24 hours per day. George Orwell would almost certainly have had long-lasting nightmares about the super-secret facility.

One of the most fascinating of all files to surface from NSA personnel is a January 2010 document with the probably pun-intended title of *Fields of Controversy*. With the lengthy subtitle of *Manipulation of Observable "Crop Circle" and Associated Phenomena for Multifaceted Gain in the Era of Terror*, it does not deal with a history of the crop circle controversy as a whole, but one specific issue of the mystery: the looming saga of 2012 and the Mayan prophecies.

The process that has led to a conclusion that something of great significance may occur in the closing days of December 2012 is a very convoluted one. It results from the Mayan Long Count Calendar, which suggests the end of a particular Earth-cycle on December 21, 2012. Or: 5,125 years after the cycle commenced. Analyses of Mayan beliefs demonstrate that the widespread notion our planet will meet its end, or that civilization will reach extinction point, on that day, is simply based on personal interpretation of the Mayan beliefs. *Nowhere* in the Mayan legends are there *any* references to the world ending or civilization collapsing in the days before 2013 dawns. Rather, it's that one word, *cycle*, that gets so many people in a state of anxiety as December 2012 gets closer.

Crop circles and 2012: a concern of the National Security Agency. (Copyright Nick Redfern.)

The Mayan civilization held to a particular belief that life on Earth exists in a series of cycles. Ours is the fourth cycle, which, the Mayans suggested, followed three previous ones in which the Gods attempted, but failed, to create a state of paradise on Earth. No one can say that we live in a blissful paradise—quite the opposite. So, does this mean we will all soon be wiped out, and life will begin anew with a fifth cycle? That's the alarming question that has many people wondering and worrying, including the National Security Agency. The reason: Many crop circle designs found in recent years seem to suggest a connection to the Mayan prophecies of impending *something*.

The NSA's Doomsday Files

A study of NSA documentation on crop circles reveals something truly astonishing: The agency's analysts carefully secured just about each and every British newspaper article ever published, suggesting a link between this predominantly English phenomenon and the 2012 debate. As an example, the appendix to the *Fields of Controversy* document contains a copy of a July 2007 article from Britain's *Daily Mail* newspaper titled "Crop Circles Are Back, and This Time They're in 3-D!" The article in question describes a then-new, gigantic, and intricate crop circle formation found near Silbury Hill in the English county of Wiltshire. Silbury Hill is a huge, prehistoric, man-made mound, the precise purpose of which is a matter of never-ending mystery to archaeologists and historians. Notably, one section of the *Daily Mail* article in the NSA report is underlined in pencil. The section in question states that Silbury Hill has been "the setting for several crop circles in the past, including an elaborate 350ft pattern featuring a giant Egyptian mosaic in the shape of two wings, surrounded by symbols which bear a striking resemblance to the Mayan Calendar which predicted that the world will end in 2012" (*Daily Mail*, 2007).

Silbury Hill, England. (Copyright Nick Redfern.)

Similarly, a June 15, 2009, article contained in Britain's *Telegraph* newspaper with the eye-catching headline of "Phoenix Crop Circle May Predict End of the World," also highlights the connections between crop circles and Armageddon-type scenarios on the horizon; this time, in relation to a huge, sculpted formation of the legendary phoenix bird that was found in a Wiltshire field. Again, we see evidence of NSA analysts underlining certain sections of the article, including the words of crop circle researcher Karen Alexander. She stated to the newspaper that the phoenix "symbolizes rebirth and a new era in many cultures across the world. Within the crop circle community many believe the designs are constantly referring to December 21 [2012] and its aftermath. This could be interpreted as the human race or earth rising again after a monumental event" (*Telegraph*, 2009).

And, as one final example of very many, only weeks after that was published, the *Daily Telegraph* spilled across its pages yet *another* story of a crop circle formation and 2012. This design, found in a field near Devizes, Wiltshire, closely resembled the traditional head-dress of the Mayans, which once again, inevitably, provoked commentary to the effect that whatever the nature behind the crop circle puzzle, it seemed to be inextricably linked to, and was intent on warning us about, what awaits us all in December 2012. Yet again, the *Daily Telegraph* chose to interview Karen Alexander, and once more the NSA carefully underlined certain of her words suggesting the appearance of this particular Mayan-themed formation was connected to the December 2012 controversy.

But why was the NSA so interested in the links between crop circles and the 2012 claims and theories? Were agency analysts in possession of secret data that confirmed some fantastic, unearthly intelligence was behind the elaborate creations, and that this same intelligence was trying to prepare us for large-scale, unmitigated disaster in the very near future? No. But NSA staff did have deep concerns about *something* in relation to crop circles, the Mayans, and December 2012. It's an issue that is as bizarre as the circular phenomenon itself.

Terror in the Fields

In 2006, and while operating alongside colleagues from their British equivalent, the Government Communications Headquarters (GCHQ), which has its base of operations in the English town of Cheltenham, and the British Police Force's elite Special Branch, NSA personnel came across the fragments of a highly unusual and very controversial rumor. Raw intelligence data, acquired by the NSA, suggested that Islamic radicals had secretly recruited human crop circle makers to create 2012-themed formations as a means to try to generate widespread Doomsday-style states of anxiety in the British populace. And the nearer we get to December 2012, so we should expect to see an increasingly growing number of Mayan-based formations in the fields of England, which, it has to be admitted, is precisely what has happened. Certainly, one only has to do a Google search on "crop circle and 2012" to understand the way in which, right now, this issue plays a significant role in crop circle research and beliefs—and also the way in which the situation creates noticeable anxiety and deep worry. As unbelievable as this all sounds, there does appear to be evidence suggesting that, regardless of whether or not the terrorist-driven theory has any actual merit to it, or was just an unproven rumor that crossed the desks of NSA analysts who felt obligated to address it, officialdom *has* investigated the possibility of a sinister Islamic link to, and manipulation of, both crop circle–themed and 2012–themed phenomena.

Matthew Williams, formerly a special investigator with the British Government's Customs & Excise agency, holds the distinction of being one of only a handful of people in the world to have been arrested, charged, and convicted for making a crop circle, although the actual crime was of causing damage to the Wiltshire, England field in which the formation was made. Back in the period of 1991 to 1999, Williams, who has a personal interest in UFOs, spent a great deal of time investigating the UFO activities of senior military personnel at a Wiltshire-based Royal Air Force base called Rudloe Manor (which we'll discuss a great deal more in a later chapter). Notably, in 1997, an office of the

British Police Force's Special Branch, operating out of Cheltenham, where GCHQ has its headquarters, began investigating Williams's Rudloe Manor-based research. The reason: There was a fear, which turned out to be wholly unfounded, that Williams was using his UFO studies as a brilliantly executed ruse to secretly collect information for the Irish Republican Army (IRA) on very sensitive, non-UFO-based work undertaken at Rudloe Manor.

That Matthew Williams was watched carefully and secretly by Cheltenham's Special Branch and specifically by Detective Sergeant Tim Camp, in 1997, in relation to the terrorist activities of the IRA, makes it all the more understandable why possibly he, among other self-confessed crop circle creators, may have been further spied upon from the mid-2000s onward while the NSA and GCHQ investigated claims that Islamic extremists were recruiting such landscape artists (as they have become known) and trying to whip up an apocalyptic frenzy in the UK in relation to 2012 fears.

It's worth noting the following words extracted from a one-page cable that was sent to NSA headquarters from personnel stationed at the American Embassy in London in 2010: "Today's terrorist-extremist holds a large number of cards and frequently brings them to the table. Exploitation of 'Crop Circle'/'2012' superstitions inserts a new 'Ace of Spades' into the Deck. Our anticipation is that summer 2012 will see the highest concentration of '2012'-biased presentations in Wilt., Eng. The response of UK tabloids and the crop circle fandom will be assessed appropriate to recommendations" (U.S. Department of State, 2010).

Even if death, disaster, and public fear do all surface on a large scale as dawn breaks on December 21, 2012, perhaps calamity will not come via the prophecies of the Mayans, which have so tangentially attracted the attention of elements of the NSA. Maybe they will result from the deranged and manipulative minds of cold-hearted terrorists for whom no area—no matter how archaic, mystical, and unexplained—is seemingly out of bounds for exploitation and utilization.

VISIONS IN THE SKIES

Exploiting the Gods

When it comes to the matter of U.S. government interest in the mysteries of the past, certainly the most controversial aspect of the entire issue revolves around the ways and means by which official agencies have exploited—or have *tried* to exploit—religious iconography as a weapon of war, deception, and manipulation. Put simply, military departments have attempted to engineer and stage-manage fantastic, religious-themed holograms and faked imagery in the skies. The reason is as astounding as it is near-unbelievable: to convince enemy personnel and hostile governments that the United States of America has God—and all of his accompanying supernatural might—on its side.

And, so the story goes today, far more darkly ambitious plans are now afoot to unleash upon the entire planet a monstrous and malignant holographic hoax relative to the so-called Second Coming. Known to conspiracy theorists as *Project Blue Beam*, it is said to be an operation designed to usher in a definitive New World Order–type society, in which the populace—duped into believing by a series of Pentagon-created aerial holograms that the final battle between good and evil is taking place in the skies above—will give up their freedoms and allow the NWO to rule them with an iron fist born out of *Old Testament*/wrath of God–style teachings.

Could such an astonishing scenario actually be true? Are there really cold-hearted people, buried deep within the corridors of power, who see the religious teachings and beliefs of the ancients as being viable ways of keeping all of us living in a state of never-ending, Hell-driven terror and martial law? To answer that question, we have to head back to the immediate years after World War II. It was during this chaotic period of recovery and rebuilding that the U.S. government began to realize how religion might play a vastly important role in both commanding and controlling the looming, and soon-to-be-growing, Cold War.

Marian Manipulation

One of the most important and relevant contributions to this particular debate is an April 14, 1950, publication of the RAND (**R**esearch **AN**d **D**evelopment) Corporation titled *The Exploitation of Superstitions for Purposes of Psychological Warfare*. Written by a RAND employee named Jean M. Hungerford, and prepared for the attention of Intelligence personnel within the U.S. Air Force, the 37-page document is an extremely interesting one and delves into some highly unusual areas, one of which has a direct bearing upon the extraordinary data contained within this particular chapter. Hungerford stated in part: "Recently a series of religious 'miracles' has been reported from Czechoslovakian villages. In one instance the cross on the altar of a parish church was reported to have bowed right and left and finally, symbolically, to the West; the 'miracle' so impressed the Czechs that pilgrims began to converge on the village from miles around until Communist officials closed the church and turned the pilgrims away from approaching roads" (Hungerford, 1950).

On another occasion, noted Hungerford, the Virgin Mary herself was said to have materialized in a vision and to have given a communist a resounding slap that knocked him unconscious! And then there was a story from Western Bohemia that made its way into Hungerford's report, which asserted locals had seen the Virgin Mary parading along the streets of a small town—with the American flag in her hand, no less—as U.S. troops and tanks followed dutifully behind.

Of course, the overriding message behind these particular visitations of the Marian kind, and reported miracles, was acutely clear: God was (a) right behind Uncle Sam; and (b) hardly a noted supporter of communism. Whether or not this was all provoked by some top secret hand of the U.S. government, of which RAND had no personal

An apparition of the Marian kind.

awareness, is unknown. But, as RAND noted in its report to the Air Force, the U.S. government had carefully, and secretly, monitored Moscow- and Czech-based radio broadcasts that discussed the claimed miracles in great depth. Most notably of all, the Russians and the Czechs exhibited deep, on-air anger and annoyance that the rumors in question were essentially casting a major slur on the entire Soviet Bloc and the communist way of life.

Hungerford noted something else that clearly demonstrated the large-scale extent to which American agents were dutifully monitoring this particular situation: "According to the Foreign Broadcast Information Services' daily reports of Soviet and Eastern European radio broadcasts, there were nine broadcasts concerning the 'miracles' between February 28 and March 19, seven from Czech transmitters and two from Moscow (including a review of a *New York Times* article on the subject)." Every response and reaction by the Soviets, it appears, was being carefully watched and analyzed (Ibid.).

In closing on this particular matter, Hungerford detailed that the Soviets had their deep suspicions that this was all some sort of religious ruse perpetrated on them by intelligence agents of America. Concerning the report of the Virgin Mary waving the Stars and Stripes, a Prague-based radio broadcaster, whose words were transcribed and translated by the CIA, said: "It is obvious at first sight that this apparition bears the mark made in the United States. These despicable machinations only help to unmask the high clergy as executors of the plans of the imperialist war-mongers communicated to them by the Vatican through its agents" (Ibid.).

It is this affair and, perhaps, this particular RAND-originated document of 1950, that galvanized America to further explore how, and under what particular circumstances, religion could be used as a tool of warfare, psychological manipulation, and control. And what a decidedly strange series of events quickly developed.

The Pentagon's Blood-Suckers

Mention the word *vampire* to most people and, depending on their age and the era in which they grew up, it will inevitably provoke a wide variety of imagery. For some, it will be 1940s–1960s memories of black-cloaked characters roaming around creepy, Eastern European gothic castles in the dead of night (deep shades of long-departed Bela Lugosi and still-active Christopher Lee, in other words). For others, it will be the watered-down *Twilight* movies, and the far more entertaining, sexually driven, bloodthirsty HBO series, *True Blood*.

Decades ago, however, vampirism was an issue that also caught the attention of the U.S. government, as did the matter of how beliefs in vampires extended way back to the civilization of ancient Babylonia, and the incredible means by which the legendary blood-suckers of old could be resurrected as part of the American military's fighting force. That's right: In a strange and convoluted way, the government of the United States of America has had vampires in its employ.

Back in the 1950s, psychological warfare planners within the American military began spreading tales of blood-sucking, monstrous vampires on the loose in the Philippines. There was, of course, reason behind this seeming madness: It was to terrify the superstitious, communist Huk rebels who, at the time, were engaged in an uprising in the

Philippines. The operation was a truly ingenious one coordinated by a certain Major General Edward Geary Lansdale. Born in 1908, Lansdale served with the U.S. Office of Strategic Services during World War II. Then, in 1945, he was transferred to HQ Air Forces Western Pacific in the Philippines, and in 1957 he received a posting to the Office of the Secretary of Defense, working as deputy assistant to the SoD for what were vaguely, but intriguingly, termed *Special Operations*. And no operation got more special than one that Lansdale pretty much singlehandedly coordinated. It was one that the likes of horror masters Stephen King, George A. Romero, and John Carpenter would surely have been infinitely proud.

At the specific request of Philippine President Elpidio Quirino, Lansdale was assigned to the Joint United States Military Assistance Group to provide assistance and guidance in the field of Intelligence, to the Philippine Army, as the latter sought to once and for all squash the Huk uprising. And it was while lending assistance to President Quirino that Lansdale had the bright and alternative idea of exploiting a local legend for psychological warfare purposes—namely, that of the deadly and monstrous Asuang Vampire, a predominantly female creature much feared for its predations throughout the Philippines for centuries. A very strange and special operation was about to begin.

In his own words, long after the affair was over and he finally felt comfortable speaking out publicly, Lansdale said: "The Huk battleground was a haunted place filled with ghosts and eerie creatures. A combat psy-war squad was brought in. It planted stories among town residents of an Asuang living on the hill where the Huks were based. Two nights later, after giving the stories time to make their way up to the hill camp, the psy-war squad set up an ambush along the trail used by the Huks" (Lansdale, 1991).

Lansdale continued that on several occasions when a Huk patrol was spied upon by U.S. military personnel, the ambushers stealthily grabbed the last man of the patrol, their quiet movements unnoticed after the sun had set and darkness had fallen upon the area. The team then did something deeply unusual and alternative: They carefully and dutifully punctured the unfortunate neck of the equally unfortunate Huk with two holes—in definitive vampire fashion—then held the body up by the heels until it was drained of most of its blood. Finally, they carefully placed the corpse of the victim where it would inevitably be stumbled upon by the Huks. When the Huks returned to look for their vanished comrade, and instead found nothing less than a blood-drained corpse, chaos and fear broke out, and the Huks exited the relevant area at high speed, vowing never to return for fear of incurring the deadly wrath of the Count Dracula–like Asuang. As a direct result of these actions, key, strategic ground was taken out of the hands of the Huk rebels.

During the 1950s, in a very strange fashion, the U.S military had vampires in its employ. (D.H. Friston, 1872.)

This is just one example of how and why a blood-sucking monster was brought to life and, arguably, how and why it deeply influenced the outcome of a military engagement, despite the fact that it never really existed in the first place. Or did it? One of the most interesting revelations of this story is that Major General Edward G. Lansdale had a very serious belief in *real* vampires: His extensive library included a copy of a 1903 book, *Devils and Evil Spirits of Babylonia* by Reginald C. Thompson, which divulged a wealth of proto-vampire-type encounters.

Moreover, Lansdale had a deep and near-obsessive fascination with the Strix, an owl-like creature prevalent in Roman and Greek folklore and history that had a maniacal thirst for human blood. On this specific issue, Lansdale's library was also home to a paper that he particularly cherished. It was titled "The Story of the Strix," and was written by Professor Samuel Grant Oliphant back in 1913. It detailed the vampiric story of the Strix legends in their full, captivating, and gory glory.

Even more notable, one of Lansdale's most beloved and repeatedly digested texts was *Ornithogonia*, penned by the Greek writer Boios, parts of which were referenced in *Metamorphoses* by Antoninus Liberalis, also a Greek writer, who lived around 100 AD. Although Boios's almost-legendary and elusive manuscript is believed by most scholars of vampirism and the Strix to be utterly and forever lost, dark legend has it that Lansdale secretly obtained a copy from a high-ranking Nazi officer two weeks after the official ending of World War II. Lansdale's only payment, after weeks of negotiation, was the promise of a 24-hour delay in reporting to his superiors the officer's whereabouts, thus allowing the war criminal a modicum of time to escape, in exchange for the ancient book. Quite rightly, Lansdale did not keep his promise and the Nazi was taken into custody immediately. As for Boios's, *Ornithogonia,* its priceless pages reportedly included details of how, and under what circumstances, legendary vampires could be called forth, conjured, and invoked, including the much-feared Greek undead drainer of blood, the Vrykolakas, and the Jewish Aluka, which, very appropriately, translates into English as "leech."

But it was not just the predatory vampires of old that Edward Lansdale let loose upon the battlefield. Incredibly, this Pentagon genius also took some of his strange inspiration from nothing less than Egyptian gods.

The Eye of the Storm

As Lansdale himself admitted long after his retirement from officialdom, a further psychological-warfare-themed operation targeted against the Huks in the 1950s involved the much-feared "Eye of God," as he termed it. In Lansdale's own words: "The name of this technique reminded me of the ancient Egyptian practice of painting watchful guardian eyes over the tombs of the Pharaohs. The painting was stylized to give the eye a baleful glare to scare away grave robbers. Recalling its appearance, I made some sketches until I recaptured the essence of its forbidding look" (Lansdale, 1991).

Lansdale continued that late at night, when the people of the Philippines had retired to their beds, U.S. military psy-war teams secretly crept into certain well-populated towns and villages and painted ominous-looking eyes upon the doors of the homes of people suspected of being associated with, and allied to, the Huks. Not surprisingly, said

Lansdale: "The mysterious presence of these malevolent eyes the next morning had a sharply sobering effect." No doubt! Rather notably, this story was noted in glowing and approving terms in a 1963 RAND paper (Ibid.).

What Lansdale was actually referring to here was the Eye of Horus, personified by Wadjet, the legendary and ancient snake-headed goddess of Lower Egypt. She was a deity that rose out of the early Egyptian city of Dep, and, along with Nekhbet, a deity originally of Upper Egypt, gave protection to the Pharaohs and the people of Egypt, particularly women about to give birth. And, just like the actions of Lansdale in the Philippines, the Eye of Horus provoked much fear in thieves, murderers, and those who might do harm to the Egyptian kings and their legacy—both in this world and in the mysterious realm of the afterlife.

How, exactly, had Lansdale come to know all this? Very simple: He owned a copy of Thomas George Allen's highly detailed and extensively footnoted *Horus in the Pyramid Texts*, a dissertation written by Allen in 1916 and published by the University of Chicago Libraries. But Lansdale still had more to come. And, it's now that we see how his work changed from that of ground-based operations to trying to perform deity-style miracles in the skies.

Castro vs. Jesus

Contained within the pages of a November 20, 1975, document titled *Alleged Assassination Plots Involving Foreign Leaders, Interim Report of the Select Committee to Study Government Operations with Respect to Intelligence Activities* is a fascinating statement from Thomas A. Parrott, who served with the CIA for 24 years, and who held the prestigious position of assistant deputy director for National Intelligence Programs.

Commenting on some of Lansdale's more bizarre operations that were prompted by religion, ancient mythology,
and legend, Parrott noted to the committee: "I'll give you
one example of Lansdale's perspicacity. He had a wonder-
ful plan for getting rid of [Fidel] Castro. This plan consisted
of spreading the word that the Second Coming of Christ
was imminent and that Christ was against Castro who was
anti-Christ. And you would spread this word around Cuba,
and then on whatever date it was, that there would be a
manifestation of this thing. And at the time—this was absolutely true—and at the time just over the horizon there
would be an American submarine that would surface off of
Cuba and send up some star-shells. And this would be the
manifestation of the Second Coming and Castro would be
overthrown" (U.S. Government Printing Office, 1975).

Star-shells are, essentially, pyrotechnic flares of the
military designed to fill the skies at night with bright and
widespread illumination. But, the ambitious plan that
Lansdale had in mind involved much more than just daz-
zling the Cubans with flares. The feasibility of using a U.S.
Navy submarine to project images of Jesus Christ onto low-
lying clouds off the coast of the Cuban capital of Havana
was also considered. The plan also involved the crew of a
U.S. military plane, camouflaged by the clouds and with its
engine significantly muffled, using powerful loudspeakers
to broadcast faked messages from an equally faked Christ
to the people of Cuba, ordering them to overthrow their
government and renounce communism.

Executed properly, such a highly alternative operation
might very well have convinced the Cubans that Jesus
Christ himself really was calling—and he was not bringing
good news for Fidel Castro. Ultimately, though the whole

thing was seen as undoubtedly ingenious in nature, it was also viewed as an operation that had a very big chance of failing catastrophically. And if the Cubans got word there was a U.S. submarine in the very immediate area and took successful military action against it, the disastrous cost in the form of American lives might have far outweighed anything that the operation could have achieved. Thus, this strange biblical charade of the Cold War was shelved.

But, it *was* briefly resurrected during the first Gulf War. This time, however, Jesus had been booted out of the picture in favor of Allah. More significantly, on this occasion, the far-simpler method of simply projecting imagery onto a cloud, searchlight-style, was to be replaced by sophisticated, hologram-based technology. Before we get to this story, there's a fascinating revelation from a UFO researcher named Ray Boeche that concerns the extent to which the U.S. government has been secretly developing hologram technology for use in warfare.

Visions in the Woods

During the final nights of December 1980, a stunning wealth of strange encounters that eerily paralleled the final minutes of Stephen Spielberg's 1977 movie, *Close Encounters of the Third Kind*, took place in a large area of British east-coast woodland called Rendlesham Forest. That the forest straddled the joint Royal Air Force/U.S. Air Force military complex of Bentwaters-Woodbridge is of deep significance: Numerous military personnel, who had been ordered into the woods after unexplained lights were seen flitting amongst the trees, comprised nearly all of the many witnesses.

What a large number of the now-retired military personnel believe they encountered in Rendlesham Forest on those long-gone nights were the manifestation and landing of a vehicle built on another world—in other words, an alien spacecraft, or a UFO. The story gets weirder and wilder with reports of dwarfish, large-headed alien entities exiting the craft, and of a huge cover-up of the affair orchestrated by the governments of the United Kingdom and the United States. But did extra-terrestrials *really* land in Rendlesham Forest more than 30 years ago?

Some have suggested that the entire event was a hologram-style experiment, tested on unwitting military personnel, to determine if they could be fooled into thinking they were encountering alien spacecraft and their otherworld crews. The purpose: to run the operation at a domestic and safe level, where the reactions and responses of the participants could be carefully watched and assessed, before unleashing something similar upon America's potential enemies.

"A Terrifying Apparition"

In late 1991, UFO investigator Ray Boeche met with two Department of Defense physicists who advised him the Rendlesham affair had nothing to do with aliens, but everything to do with highly advanced terrestrial technology. Boeche reflected as follows on the words of his two whistleblowers: "They said there was a sense that this was maybe, in some sense, staged. That some of the senior people there were more concerned with the reaction of the men—how they responded to the situation, rather than what was actually going on. That this was some sort of psychotronic device, a hologram, to see what sort of havoc they can wreak with people. But even if it was a type of hologram, they said it could interact with the environment. The tree marks and the pod marks at the landing site were indications of that. But how can you have a projected thing like a hologram that also has material, physical capabilities? They wouldn't elaborate on this" (Redfern, 2010).

Jenny Randles is a British-based UFO researcher and writer who met with Boeche in Lincoln, Nebraska, in 1992, during which the discussion turned the allegations that the Rendlesham affair was born out of secret, sophisticated experimentation, rather than alien visitation. After speaking with Boeche, Randles recorded that of the technology involved, it "supposedly stimulated the mind into having vivid hallucinations but, at the same time, created physical effects in the real world which could take on a semblance of the appearance of the hallucinated images. In other words, what was seen was mostly in the mind—and certainly a production of the subconscious imagination—but it was not entirely without physical form and partially substantial in the same way that a hologram is real, but has no weight or solidity. The result is a terrifying apparition" (Randles, 1998).

If Boeche's DoD sources were being honest with him (an issue that, admittedly, remains somewhat unclear) then we may have evidence to support the rumor that this technology was going to be used during the first Gulf War of 1990–1991, or, at least until someone pulled the plug on the operation. And, just as was the case with Edward Lansdale's operations in the Philippines in the mid-1950s and Cuba in the early-1960s, the U.S. government took its inspiration from ancient teachings and holy books. Interestingly, the very people who planned the operation were attached to the U.S. Air Force, whose personnel were involved in the 1980 encounters at Rendlesham Forest, England.

The idea sounds like something straight out of the domain of science fiction. This, however, was amazing science fact. It involved a massively ambitious plan to position a gigantic mirror in near-Earth orbit that would reflect, right over Baghdad, the capital of Iraq, a gigantic image of Allah, to try to influence and manipulate the Iraqis via religious imagery. There was also a plan to have the image of Allah speak to the Iraqi people. Such an incredible act would be achieved via the use of fringe technology designed to beam voices directly into people's heads.

Hearing Voices

The Defense Advanced Research Projects Agency (DARPA) has admitted to working on a program designed to perfect what it calls the Sonic Projector. Of this particular operation, DARPA says: "The goal of the Sonic Projector program is to provide Special Forces with a method of surreptitious audio communication at distances over 1 km. Sonic Projector technology is based on the non-linear interaction of sound in air translating an ultrasonic signal into audible sound. The Sonic Projector will be designed to be a man-deployable system, using high power acoustic transducer technology and signal processing algorithms which result in no, or unintelligible, sound everywhere but at the intended target. The Sonic Projector system could be used to conceal communications for special operations forces and hostage rescue missions and to disrupt enemy activities" (Defense Technical Information Center, 2009).

The stark and terrifying reality is that hearing voices in one's head may not be a sign of mental illness. It may be the result of careful Pentagon profiling and targeting—which is precisely what was planned for in Iraq during the first Gulf War. So, why was the operation halted? Perhaps the technology, both visual and acoustic, was not quite as ready for deployment as might have been hoped for by the Air Force. But there was another reason, too: Showing imagery of Allah is specifically outlawed in Islamic teachings. Therefore, projecting an image of Allah to the people of Baghdad would have had no meaningful effect, as those same people were not overly conversant with artistic renditions of Allah in the first place.

But 1991 was more than two decades ago. Maybe, today, things have changed and the technical problems have finally been ironed out. Welcome to *Project Blue Beam*.

Devilish Deception

Project Blue Beam, according to conspiracy theorists, is a clandestine program that is designed to control the world's population by ensuring the fulfillment of certain biblical, end-times prophecies through stage-managed fakery and elaborate holograms. So the dark theories go, numerous, sophisticated, space-based, laser-generating satellites in near-Earth orbit will—in the near future—simultaneously project images of an entire range of gods and deities, including Mohammed, Krishna, Jesus Christ, and Buddha—to each and every corner of our planet.

Those same images will then combine into one entity dreaded by all: the Antichrist, who—in thunderous tones—will reveal to the shocked human race that all the many and varied scriptures, legends, stories, and texts of a religious nature faithfully studied throughout human history have been wholly misunderstood, and are the sole cause of conflict on our ever-warring world. The Antichrist will then assert that, in view of this, all earthly religions must be discarded in favor of a brand new religion—with him at its helm, of course.

Those who have studied the *Project Blue Beam* data have suggested this situation will result in worldwide panic, civil disorder, and the disintegration of society at a shockingly quick rate—that is, until a New World Order surfaces and (with the help of its many secret minions within the United Nations, and inside the military and police of numerous nations) enslaves the world's population under the might of either the *real* Antichrist, or a powerful figure within the NWO intent on controlling everyone's future by *posing* as the Antichrist. A variation on this theme suggests that *Project Blue Beam* will be used to plunge each and every one of us into a dark age controlled by power-crazed Old Testament–type zealots with nothing but unending manipulation and whole-scale enslavement on their insane minds. Or, at least, that is what the rumors on the Internet tell us is going to happen.

The first thought of most people would surely be to dismiss such controversial theorizing as nothing more than a distasteful April Fool's Day joke taken to—or even way beyond—its ultimate extreme. But, as we have seen, for more than half a century, elements of the U.S. military *have* sought to influence not just governments, but whole cultures, too, via stage-managed, fabricated events of a religious nature that were, in turn, influenced by the ancient cultures and beliefs of Babylonia and Egypt. *Project Blue Beam*, then, may well be a 21st-century, worldwide equivalent of Edward Lansdale's ambitious plans to have a bogus Jesus Christ appear in the skies of early-1960s Cuba.

DJINN,
STAR-GATES,
AND IMMORTALITY

Definitively paranormal in nature, Djinn are integral figures within the teachings and beliefs of Islam, who feature extensively within the *Qur'an*, and who are said to inhabit a strange and twilight realm that co-exists with and sometimes crosses paths with ours—or, another dimension, one might be very much inclined to suggest. Whereas we are purely flesh and blood, however, the all-powerful Djinn are the product of flame and fire, and they can be as playful and benevolent as they can be malevolent and downright deadly. Some Djinn are widely believed to be possessed by an overriding and near-psychotic hatred of the human race. It is that same hatred that is said to provoke Djinn to torment, manipulate, and deceive us as the mood and moment take them.

Nevertheless, Djinn—from whom the more well-known term *Genie* is derived, and which translates as "to hide or be hidden"—are said to possess a number of surprisingly human-like traits: There are both male and female Djinn, they have families, they mourn their dead, and, just like the human race, they possess free will. On this latter point, so the legend goes, when Iblis, a legendary Djinn viewed today as the Islamic equivalent of the Christian Devil, chose to exploit that same free will and refused to bow down to Adam after being ordered to do so by Allah, he was summarily ejected from Paradise. Djinn are said to haunt remote locales, including caves, valleys, mountains, labyrinthine tunnels, and desert wastelands. In addition, they have the ability to shape-shift into a wide range of forms, including winged monsters of a gargoyle-style nature, spectral black dogs, and writhing snake-like entities. They're hardly, then, the sort of entities one might be inclined to hang out with, unless one is attached to select and secret arms of the U.S. Government, as we shall now see.

Dimension-Hopping Djinn and the Military

In 1995, anomalies researcher Philip Imbrogno made a trip to Saudi Arabia, during the course of which he learned of secret, long-term attempts by an elite, covert unit of the U.S. military to actually try to capture Djinn. The purpose of the risk-filled program (Imbrogno was told by official sources) was to secure for the U.S. government a highly advanced technological device that permitted Djinn to pass through solid matter and also through what were intriguingly described as dimensional windows. It scarcely needs mentioning that if such phenomenal technology does exist, then the possible outcome of its use as a tool of the military could be near-incalculable.

To what extent such an operation was successful, Imbrogno did not find out, unfortunately. If such an extraordinary goal *had* been achieved, however, Imbrogno was advised in no uncertain terms that the findings would undoubtedly have been classified at an extremely high level. Similarly, while visiting Oman on the same trip, Imbrogno heard a story of the governments of Oman and the United States both having an awareness of Djinn reality, and even trying to make some form of deal with them. Surely no one needs to be told that such an action would be disastrous. But try telling that to the government.

Seeking out the Star-Gate

The events and data discussed thus far have—for the most part, anyway—been focused upon 20th century-based governmental explorations of the mysteries of the distant past. Testimony and data, however, suggest that such clandestine research is still very much ongoing in the 21st century. Many of the latter-day claims, which are undeniably even more controversial and extreme than anything we have previously addressed, are focused upon the nature and intent of the War on Terror and the reasoning behind the 2003 invasion of Iraq. Put simply, there is a growing body of conspiracy-based researchers that believes the Iraq War had very little to do with a quest to seek out Saddam Hussein's ever-elusive weapons of mass destruction, or even to uncover ways to secretly exert firm control over the flow and direction of Middle Eastern oil. Rather, the escalating belief is that Iraq is home to ancient secrets and technologies that the United States would dearly and secretly like to get its eager hands on. True or not, let's see what is being said and who is saying it.

In 2003, the same year that the Iraq War began, wild and dark rumors began to surface on the Internet suggesting there was a distinctly covert agenda behind the invasion of Iraq, one that was just about as far away from oil and WMDs as was humanly possible. The tale, which was largely publicized by Michael Salla, author of *Islamic Radicalism, Muslim Nations and the West*, was that, at some undetermined point before the invasion, elements of the Bush administration learned that secreted deeply somewhere in central Iraq was a very old technological marvel known as a star-gate. In simple terms, it was described as being a portal or doorway that could allow the user to travel, near-instantaneously, from our world to another, and vice-versa, like a highly futuristic equivalent of the New York subway system, one might be inclined to say. It must also be said that this sounds very much like the story told to Philip Imbrogno, while he was in Saudi Arabia in 1995, that the U.S. military was on the hunt for a highly advanced technological device that permitted Djinn to pass through what were described as dimensional windows.

If the sensational story of the star-gate has some degree of truth to it, then who built it? Certainly not Saddam Hussein, that's for sure. The rumor mill suggested that the creators were none other than the legendary Anunnaki, which translates as those who came to Earth from Heaven. And, considerable millennia ago, they reportedly arrived on Earth at Sumer, located in southern Mesopotamia, between the Tigris and Euphrates rivers, and parts of what is, today, southern Iraq. The Anunnaki were perceived as powerful gods by the people of Sumer, whose society, science, agriculture, and technology were all said to have been significantly transformed and upgraded, almost overnight, by the presence of their near-magical overlords from the skies above. Not everyone was convinced the Anunnaki were literal gods, however. In 1976, ancient astronaut authority Zecharia Sitchin concluded the Anunnaki were superpowerful, visiting extra-terrestrials. After leaving their mark on Sumerian culture and history in distant antiquity, we are told, the Anunnaki exited the Earth, never to come back—until now, or very soon, perhaps.

As for why the star-gate was built, the story was that the Anunnaki inhabit a world called Nibiru, whose orbit is so vast that it only enters our solar system once approximately every 3,600 years. And, yes, you guessed right: Nibiru, the supporters of this theory assure us, is now, finally, on its way back, as are the Anunnaki. So we are told, the star-gate will permit the Anunnaki to step into our world once more, in much the same way they did all those thousands of years ago.

This, sources maintain, was not at all what the United States wanted to hear, because it had the potential to completely derail the plans of cold, emotionless, and powerful characters around the world that wished, and *still* dearly wish, to see the human race eventually controlled under the auspices of an all-encompassing New World Order of Orwellian proportions. So, the battle was on for the United States to locate and take control of the star-gate before the Anunnaki staged their triumphant return.

But, if the story of the star-gate was real, then where, precisely, was it located? One theory suggested deep below a very ancient, man-made structure on a river called the Little Zab, which runs from Iran's Zagros Mountains to the Tigris. Another possibility was an incredibly old crypt underneath a Sumerian ziggurat (or step-pyramid-type creation) at Dur-Kurigalzu. Around 19 miles from Baghdad, it was built in the 14th century by King Kurigalzu I of the near-Eastern people, the Kassites, and, admittedly, might have been an ideal place to secret such an incredible device.

There were other rumors, too. Michael Salla noted that, of stories suggesting the star-gate was buried within a secure location at Uruk, a very early Sumerian city, there were intriguing developments. Whether the star-gate story has merit or not, it is a fact that in 2002 a team of German archaeologists was granted permission to dig in that very area, ostensibly to further our knowledge of the ancient history of the region and its people in relation to matters of a wholly down-to-earth, historical, and archaeological nature.

Salla, however, was not quite so sure that was *all* that was going on: "Given the prominence of Uruk and its likelihood as the site for a Sumerian Stargate, then resumption of excavations raises questions over why they were resumed at this time and what is being sought." He added that there may have been significant, hidden reasons for "what on the surface appears to be a purely scientific dig of an ancient Sumerian capital" (Salla, 2003).

Rumors also circulated that certain data pertaining to the star-gate, to the Anunnaki, and to their return, was secretly held at the Baghdad-based National Museum of Iraq—which housed numerous priceless, ancient artifacts dating back more than 5,000 years, and which were representative of many cultures and people who have inhabited Mesopotamia throughout significant millennia. That the museum was summarily plundered and looted between

April 10 and 12, 2003 by sources not entirely clear, provoked theories that some of those who were responsible were secretly searching for, and duly found, data and materials that would help in the concerted effort to uncover the secret location of the star-gate.

Certainly, in the build-up to the Iraq War, the American Council for Cultural Policy, astutely anticipating the chaos that would surely ensue when battle commenced, practically pleaded with the Pentagon to provide some degree of protection to the museum and its historically important contents from potential thieves. No such assurance was made, however, which also heightened the theories that the raids were pre-planned and had ulterior motives that extended far beyond a bunch of stragglers just trying to make a bit of money off of a few old Sumerian antiques. Whatever the truth of the matter, numerous priceless items from the very earliest years of Sumerian, Mesopotamian, and Iraqi culture vanished, never to be seen again; whether or not any of those same items were used in a search for the theoretical star-gate, however, remains unknown.

And that, pretty much, is where things stand to this day: Nibiru is yet to return, the star-gate (if it even existed at all) has seemingly not been reopened, and neither the Anunnaki nor the New World Order is running the planet—yet.

The Gods' Gold

Jim Marrs, one of the world's leading experts in the field of conspiracy theories, has suggested an additional reason that may have prompted the invasion of Iraq. It deals with something that has become known as White Powder Gold, a product of ancient alchemy that may possess astonishing attributes. Marrs has theorized that White Powder Gold may very possibly have been the mysterious, white, powdery substance that has become famously known as Manna. Fashioned into small cakes or boiled, Manna is said to have sustained the Israelites during their exodus from Egypt, demonstrating its health-giving and life-saving properties.

The gathering of Manna.
(Copyright James Tissot, 1896.)

It has also been theorized that White Powder Gold was the enigmatic product referred to in the *Egyptian Book of the Dead* as the Bread of Presence. It was a mystery-steeped food item, possibly providing both physical and spiritual nourishment, ingested by the Pharaohs while making ritualistic journeys into the afterlife, and that was said to have been extracted from gold via the use of nothing less than definitive alchemy, the ancient, near-magical science of transmuting base metals into just about whatever the secrets of alchemy might allow for. And in relation to gold, it has been claimed that certain ancient, alchemic experimentation stumbled upon something truly sensational.

Who Wants to Live Forever?

Legend suggests that White Powder Gold can do far more than just nourish the body and offer medicinal treatment. It is said to possess the ability to rejuvenate organs, cells, blood, and the very DNA that defines who we are, as individuals and, collectively, as a species. And, that rejuvenation may be unending. White Powder Gold might very well be the key to literal immortality.

Interestingly, centuries-old stories of life-extending elixirs, derived from alchemic techniques, can be found all over the world. It was the belief of Chinese alchemists, for example, that downing a mysterious potion of alchemically altered jade or mercury could offer the imbiber immortality or, at the very least, a massively extended lifespan. Early Indian folklore has its own immortality-inducing cocktail, too. It is known as Amrita. Then there are the likes of the biblical Noah and Methuselah. The former is said to have lived for 950 years, while the latter, we are informed, walked the Earth for 969 years. Could it be the case that the ancients knew something of alchemy and immortality, an incredible secret that, today, is long-lost, but that certain powerful players in the government might want to uncover and harness for their own selfish ends? Jim Marrs certainly doesn't rule out such a possibility.

Back in 1999, archaeological excavations undertaken around 100 miles from Baghdad uncovered an astonishingly large number of priceless items dating back to Sumerian times. A number of those items were linked to the legendary King Gilgamesh, the fifth king of Uruk, who is said to have reigned for approximately 120 years, around 2,500 to 2,400 BC, thus demonstrating that he, too, had achieved an extraordinarily long lifespan, which was also attributed to alchemical means. And to where were these amazing new discoveries taken? To none other than the Baghdad-based National Museum of Iraq, which, as noted, was looted in 2003, possibly with deliberate, covert intent.

Is it possible that the thievery that went on at the museum when war broke out was not simply a by-product of the chaos and disorder that inevitably falls upon any turbulent war zone? Might there have been certain parties in the U.S. government that were dead-set on securing any and all data that could have shed significant light on the nature of immortality, alchemy, and how Gilgamesh lived for such an incredible period of time? If the archaeological findings of 1999 did offer answers to such incredible questions, then the looting of the museum may not have been done in a wholly random fashion at all, Marrs maintains. Instead, it might have been a very carefully orchestrated operation. Evidence does suggest that those who plundered the museum of some of its many and varied secrets planned ahead, knew precisely what they were looking for, and even knew exactly where to find it.

In the aftermath of the widespread pillaging of the National Museum of Iraq, Colonel Matthew Bogdanos of the U.S. Marine Corps was assigned to lead an investigation into the matter.

In early 2004, Colonel Bogdanos said of the losses from the museum, that 40 exhibits had been taken from the public gallery, of which, at the time, 11 had been found. As far as the museum's storage rooms were concerned, more than 3,000 items were removed by looters. Fortunately, most of those items were subsequently recovered. But, it's what Bogdanos had to say about the museum's basement area that is most provocative of all: "...it is inconceivable to me that the basement was breached and the items stolen without an intimate insider's knowledge of the museum. From there about 10,000 pieces were taken. We've only recovered 650, approximately" (Archaeological Institute of America, 2004).

Might some of those still-missing items from the museum's basement have been relative to the story of Gilgamesh, immortality, and White Powder Gold? To offer at least a degree of an answer to that question, it is perhaps apposite to cite the words of Jim Marrs himself, who says that "the ages-long quest for both gold and its alchemical secrets, ancient texts that speak of life-giving powder and the proximity of Iraq to the source of knowledge concerning this certainly provides one possible motive for the invasion and looting of Iraq" (Marrs, 2004).

One final point on this strange story: You will recall that back in 1947, elements of the CIA took careful, secret interest in certain Dead Sea Scrolls and ancient texts that were focused upon the Book of Daniel. As noted, the Book of Daniel is filled with stories of Daniel's weird visions and dreams. Many of those visions and dreams took place during Daniel's time in Babylon at the court of the legendary king Nebuchadnezzar II, who ruled over the Neo-Babylonian Empire from 605 BC to 562 BC, and who consulted Daniel on the nature and meaning of his (Nebuchadnezzar II's) very own dreams and nightmares. It so transpires that Saddam Hussein considered himself to be nothing less than the literal reincarnation of Nebuchadnezzar II. If Hussein, who was massively knowledgeable on the life, history, and folklore of Nebuchadnezzar II, was in possession of certain ancient secrets of the same type that seemed to occupy the CIA back in 1947, this might be an indication of yet another reason why Iraq was targeted for invasion: to secure those same secrets.

And now, with the strange and extensive role played by the U.S. government in relation to ancient artifacts, archaeological mysteries, and the puzzles of the distant past carefully dissected and assessed, it's time to address the matter of what certain other nations may know about matters secret, sensational, archaeological, and archaic.

SEEKING
ANCIENT
ARTIFACTS

The Possession of Hitler

Without any shadow of doubt, the United States aside, the one body of people whose research and investigations into the field of ancient mysteries reached ambitious and controversial heights, was the Nazis. A great deal of that which has been written about such issues, however, is either exaggeration, historically inaccurate, or plain distortion. Nevertheless, there are some startling nuggets of truth in wartime Germany's interest in the mysteries of the past that cry out for both attention and commentary.

To do so, we have to first go back to 1925. It was in this year that a certain Dr. Ernst Schertel sent a copy of his 1923 book, *Magic: History, Theory, and Practice*, to none other than the one man who was responsible for plunging the world into a state of chaos and death between 1939 and 1945: Adolf Hitler. Evidently, Hitler was deeply intrigued and impressed by Schertel's book. Hitler carefully read the book, and underlined and marked certain passages and sentences that caught his attention. One underlined section read: "He who does not have the demonic seed within himself will never give birth to a magical world." While a second stated: "Satan is the beginning." This was an ominous and unsettling precursor to the bloodshed that enveloped the world only a few short years later (Schertel, 2009).

Interestingly, August Kubizek, one of Adolf Hitler's closest friends since childhood, maintained that, even in his teens, Hitler had confidently predicted he would return Germany to its earlier glories and duly make it the dominant nation on the planet. Rather unsettlingly, Kubizek recalled that, at times, it seemed as if during his near-maniacal rants Hitler was possessed by some mysterious occult entity that used the Nazi leader as a vessel for its plots and plans on the world arena. In relation to this issue, some people have suggested that maybe Hitler was literally possessed by evil supernatural forces. Father Gabriele Amorth, a Roman Catholic priest, and a skilled and experienced exorcist of the Diocese of Rome, is personally convinced that the Nazis were "all possessed." He adds: "All you have to do is think about what Hitler—and Stalin—did. Almost certainly they were possessed by the Devil" (Pisa, 2006).

The Holy Grail

Just like the power-crazed Adolf Hitler himself, a large number of senior Nazis, including Richard Walther Darré,

Rudolf Hess, Otto Rahn, and Heinrich Himmler, exhibited deep and unrelenting obsessions with issues relative to ancient artifacts, mystical legends, and the dark domain of all things supernatural and paranormal. Rahn was a classic case: He rose to a position of power in an arm of Nazi-Germany's greatly feared SS, and spent a wealth of time researching and searching for the so-called Holy Grail, which, Christian teachings tell us, was the plate or cup that was used by Jesus at the legendary Last Supper.

That the Holy Grail was said to possess extraordinary powers, pushed the Nazis on even more in their attempts to find this fantastic phenomenon, and then command those same powers as weapons of war against the Allies. Thankfully, the plans of the Nazis did not see the light of day. The Holy Grail remained out of the hands of Rahn, the SS, and Hitler, and the Western world was not decimated by the mysterious might of God. But, this didn't stop the Nazis from pursuing other ancient and controversial avenues.

Ahnenerbe Obsessions

Widely acknowledged by many World War II historians as being the ultimate driving force behind the Nazi's research into religious items of alleged awesome power, Heinrich Himmler was, perhaps, the one high-ranking official in the Third Reich most obsessed with the domain of the occult. In July 1935, Himmler, along with Richard Walther Darre and Dr. Herman Wirth, became a key player in the establishment of the Ahnenerbe, which was the ancestral heritage division of the SS. Interestingly, Himmler had a curious obsession: He believed the Aryans had their origins in the legendary land of Atlantis that so obsessed Edgar Cayce, whose Virginia Beach–based foundation was infiltrated by the CIA in the early 1960s.

One of the primary goals of the Ahnenerbe was to prove that many early civilizations were seeded, and their fantastic architecture was constructed by ancient Nordics, the very same ones that Himmler believed were the Atlanteans. Or, as the Ahnenerbe interpreted things: The original rulers of the planet from whom the elite of the Nazis could claim their personal lineage and heritage.

Of some note, in 1939, the Ahnenerbe planned to investigate and excavate in the mountains of Bolivia, as part of their quest to prove the existence of a very old Aryan super-race. Bolivia, we have seen, was a nation with which Morris K. Jessup exhibited significant obsessions of the ancient astronaut variety. The project was largely prompted by the work of a German archaeologist named Edmund Kiss, who was the author of a book titled *The Last Queen of Atlantis*. Like so many within the SS, which he duly joined after war broke out, Kiss was obsessed with the idea that the Aryans had seeded a worldwide civilization in an ancient era.

In the latter years of the 1920s, Kiss traveled to Tiwanaku, Bolivia, a pre-Incan site rich in archaeological importance with which Morris K. Jessup was fascinated. Contrary to the beliefs of conventional history and archaeology, Kiss believed that some of the fantastic structures of the Bolivians were actually built as far back as 17,000 BC by superior Nordic races. And it was this theory that prompted a planned SS-sponsored trek to the Bolivian mountains in 1939. The project, however, was permanently derailed when, in September of that year, the Nazis invaded Poland, Britain declared war on Germany, and Hitler was forced to divert much-needed manpower, resources, and money elsewhere.

The Spear of Destiny

Trevor Ravenscroft, an investigative author, spent years pursuing the strange story of the links between Nazi Germany and the fabled Roman spear or lance that supposedly pierced the body of Jesus during the crucifixion—the Spear of Destiny, as it is most famously known. Ravenscroft's research, which is disputed by some scholars of the Nazi war-machine and its occult links, suggested that Hitler deliberately instigated World War II with the intention of trying to secure the spear, with which he was said to be overwhelmingly fascinated, to the point of near-obsession. So Ravenscroft's account told it, however, Hitler catastrophically failed. Ravenscroft suggested that as World War II neared its end, and when Nazi Germany was facing overwhelming defeat at the hands of the Allies, the Spear of Destiny fell into the possession of U.S. General George Smith Patton, Jr. According to legend, losing the spear would result in death—a prophecy that that was said to have been definitively fulfilled when Hitler committed suicide in 1945.

The Ark of the Covenant

Referenced in the Holy Bible's Book of Exodus as the repository for the so-called Tablets of Stone on which the Ten Commandments were prepared, the Ark of the Covenant was a truly mysterious creation. Reportedly, it was constructed to the careful, specific instructions of God, as related to Moses while on Mount Sinai. Those perceived by God as being capable of performing the task of building the Ark were Bezalel and Oholiab. While in-depth background data on the pair are sorely lacking, the former is described in religious texts as being of the tribe of Judah, the son of

Hur, and a colleague of Moses. The latter, meanwhile, is identified as the son of Ahisamakh, of the tribe of Dan.

Reportedly made out of shittim-wood—the wood of what today is called the Red Acacia tree—the Ark was plated with gold, and four rings of gold were affixed to its feet. Sat atop the Ark was a cover, also of gold, known as the Mercy Seat, which displayed imagery of supernatural religious entities, or cherubim, as they are termed. When completed, the Ark was approximately 45 inches in length, 27 inches in width, and 27 inches in height. As for its purpose, well, that is a matter of deep intrigue.

The Ark of the Covenant was said to possess some deadly powers.

The Ark of the Covenant appears to have acted as a vessel that allowed God to speak directly with whomever was deemed worthy and necessary. In simple terms, it acted like a two-way radio. Some have said that this may have been *exactly* what it was. But it was supposedly far more than just a device of cosmic communication.

The Holy Bible states that during the course of the Israelites' exodus from Egypt, priests held the Ark aloft, but at a distance of a minimum of 2,000 cubits, or approximately a half-mile in modern-day terminology, from the huge body of people that was steadily on the move. One could make the argument that there seemed to have been something curious about the Ark of the Covenant that suggested close proximity to it might have proved distinctly hazardous to human health and well-being, unless one was conversant with the instructions of God. Certainly, the Ark of the Covenant was said to be a device of impressive qualities: First, it apparently had the ability to push aside the waters of the River Jordan, thus allowing the Israelites to cross without the fear of drowning (shades of the legendary parting of the Red Sea). Second, in around 1400 BC, the Israelites were said to have successfully destroyed the huge wall of Jericho, a city situated near the River Jordan in Palestinian territories, by walking around its massive perimeter for seven days with the Ark of the Covenant held high and pointing directly toward the wall. Then, on the final day, numerous trumpets made of ram's horn were blown in the direction of the wall, resulting in its complete collapse. Might, perhaps, this story of magical trumpets actually have been a distorted legend of ancient acoustic technology employed not to raise massive stones, as per the pyramids of Egypt possibly, but, instead, to bring them crashing to the ground? If nothing else, it's an intriguing theory upon which to muse.

But of one thing many researchers have become convinced: that the Ark of the Covenant was a device of technological, rather than godly, proportions. Ark commentator Paul Schroeder says enough evidence exists to suggest the Ark of the Covenant was created as an "alien transmitter-capacitor" and as a form of weapon. Schroeder adds: "One of the Gold plates was positively charged and one was negatively charged and together they formed the condenser. If one of the cherubims positioned above the Mercy Seat acted as a magnet, then one has the rudimentary requirements of a two way communication set" (Schroeder, 2010).

Also, the voice of creation behind the Ark warned those that might have come into its proximity to wear specific items of clothing and to specifically avoid others. Schroeder concludes that such warnings may have been delivered to lessen the possibility of electrocution. Certainly, the Holy Bible contains a number of accounts of people touching the Ark and being instantly killed. Religious scholars say the deaths were provoked by the power of God. Others suggest by electricity surging through the body of an unfortunately ungrounded individual (Ibid.).

Whether the work of God, aliens, or ancient man displaying surprisingly advanced knowledge of electricity, one thing we know for sure about the Ark of the Covenant: Adolf Hitler sorely wanted it. This is hardly surprising, as it could part mighty waters, flatten whole city walls, and kill in an instant. In the wrong hands, then, the Ark had the dire potential of being the ultimate weapon of mass destruction.

Hitler is known to have ordered the Ahnenerbe to seek out the Ark of the Covenant. Deeply problematic, however, was the fact that Nazi Germany was racing to find the Ark while also fighting a war against much of Western Europe, the Soviet Union, and the United States of America. In addition, the Ark had reportedly vanished centuries earlier, and was now—depending on who one believed—carefully and secretly guarded somewhere in France, Jordan, Italy, Africa, or Ireland, among other areas of the world. Thus, with resources shrinking, and with the Nazi empire crumbling in the face of increasing Allied attacks, Hitler's plans to secure the Ark of the Covenant failed. They were, however, forever immortalized in Steven Spielberg's 1981 movie *Raiders of the Lost Ark*, which saw Harrison Ford's Indiana Jones character preventing the Nazis from obtaining the Ark and using it against the Allies. In the movie, the Ark ends up in a secret U.S. government building, locked far away from inquiring eyes and minds.

American Parallels

As a brief aside on the same subject of the Ark of the Covenant and the U.S. government, H.P. Albarelli, Jr., cited earlier in the pages of this book, has referred to "keen interest in the Ark of the Covenant" displayed by the CIA, as well as a fascination for the "rock at Horeb" (Albarelli, Jr., 2009).

The latter is a reference to Mount Horeb, where, according to the Book of Deuteronomy in the Hebrew Bible, Moses received the Ten Commandments from God. And although some biblical students perceive Mount Horeb and Mount Sinai to be one and the same, a significant number of scholars most certainly do not. Thus, we may never know for sure precisely where Moses allegedly received the legendary commandments.

One of the tales attached to the story of Mount Horeb is that when the Israelites were in the wilderness and perilously short of fresh drinking water, Moses supposedly climbed the mountain and struck a particular piece of rock, which cracked open and—lo and behold—water came pouring out, thus saving the Israelites from otherwise-certain death by dehydration. It was this story, says Albarelli, that prompted the CIA to investigate the controversial issue of dowsing, the search for water by unconventional (some might conclude even supernatural) means.

Though it may sound strange to suggest the CIA has taken an interest in dowsing, this is most certainly the case. In 1978, staff at the Foreign Technology Division (FTD) at Wright-Patterson Air Force Base, in Dayton, Ohio, prepared an extensive paper titled *Paraphysics R&D – Warsaw Pact*. (R&D referring to Research and Development). Page 23 of the document details positive results of both U.S. and Soviet research in the field of dowsing. Notably, a copy of the entire FTD document was sent to the CIA's Office of Science and Technology (OSI) shortly after its publication. It's worth noting, too, that within the Hebrew Bible, 1 Kings 8:9 identifies the Ark of the Covenant as containing the Tablets of Stone given to Moses on Mount Horeb and that were inscribed with the Ten Commandments.

Thus, we see several issues that inextricably linked the CIA's quest with that of Adolf Hitler, including the Ten Commandments, an interest in dowsing (which, arguably, is what Moses achieved on the mount, whether Sinai or Horeb), and—firmly leading the pack—the Ark of the Covenant.

The Other Ark

There was an additional ark that also attracted the interest of Adolf Hitler. It was a very different type of ark from the Ark of the Covenant, however. It's one we have already encountered in our strange journey into the past. If you have not yet guessed, it is Noah's Ark. Exactly why the Nazis wished to locate and retrieve the Ark of Noah from its reported resting place on Turkey's Mount Ararat is unfortunately very far from clear. But, they most certainly did try to locate and recover it. Files that originated with Britain's Secret Intelligence Service (SIS) confirm such extraordinary facts. The papers in question date from 1948, three years after the war was over, but tell of intriguing interviews with captured Nazi scientists brought to the United States in the immediate post-war era via a secret operation known as *Paperclip*.

The SIS data reveals that in the latter days of World War II, elements of the German military were planning to fly a sophisticated spy-balloon, based upon radical, Japanese designs, over Mount Ararat, as part of a careful and concerted effort to locate Noah's Ark and plunder certain strange secrets (never really explained or detailed) that the Ahnenerbe believed remained hidden within the depths of its aged hull.

Such a scenario is not at all out of bounds. The Japanese, who were closely allied with Nazi Germany during World II—and particularly so after their bombing of Pearl Harbor in 1941—were master builders of advanced and unusual balloons. Arguably one of the best-kept secrets of World War II, the Balloon-Bomb—or *Fugo* as it was generally referred—was a classified weapon constructed and flown by the Japanese military. Nine thousand such devices were built and employed against the United States.

More than 10 meters in diameter when inflated, the balloons were constructed out of paper or rubberized silk, and carried below them payloads of small bombs that were powerful enough to wreak significant tragedy and havoc if stumbled upon at the wrong moment. They were intensively launched from the east coast of Honshu during a six-month period beginning in the latter part of 1944, and traveled more than 6,000 miles eastward across the Pacific to North America. The vast majority of the Fugos failed to reach their planned targets, but U.S. Army estimates suggested 1,000 made it to the States, the majority having come down in such West Coast states as Oregon and Washington, and some in British Columbia.

So, knowing what we do about its skills in such realms, the government of Japan may very well have assisted its German partners in trying to find Noah's Ark. And, providing them with some form of highly advanced, sturdy reconnaissance balloon that could have been flown over Mount Ararat seems not so unusual. Although the available SIS records are woefully incomplete on this issue (perhaps *suspiciously* incomplete) they do demonstrate that a strange Nazi quest to find Noah's Ark did go ahead. Fortunately, as with all of the plans of Hitler and the Ahnenerbe, the search for the legendary ship came to a crashing end. In 1945, Hitler's hordes were finally defeated, and the man himself took the cowardly way out of choosing death by his own hand.

Nazi Germany's search for the mysteries of the ancient world was now as dead as the Fuhrer himself. But there is yet another nation that, just like both the United States and Germany, has investigated such issues—and in deep secrecy, too.

THE DANCING STONES
OF ENGLAND

In the same way that we have seen clear and undeniable evidence of massive U.S. government interest in ancient sites, artifacts, myths, and legends, very much the same can be said about the activities of the British government. And that same interest appears to have been predominantly focused on three particular locations of deep archaeological renown: Avebury and Stonehenge, both situated in the county of Wiltshire, and the Rollright Stones of Oxfordshire.

The Avebury Formation

The mysterious stones of Avebury, England. (Copyright Nick Redfern.)

Avebury is one of the most captivating prehistoric earthworks in all of Europe. The initial phase of the construction, of what amounts to a trio of stone circles, began around 2600 BC and involved the excavation of the ditches, or the Henge, as it is also known. Estimates suggest that there were originally 400 standing stones within the Henge.

Having been transported to the area (by rollers, some say), the stones were positioned into specific locations marked by chalk, and the process of erecting them using stakes duly began. The original layout was of an outer circle that encompassed the inside of the Henge and consisted of 98 stones, and within this circle were constructed two more circles, both with the same diameter. As for who exactly built the complex, that is a very difficult question to answer: An indigenous tribe, visiting Native Americans, the comrades and followers of the legendary King Arthur (the remains of whom, a few Arthurian scholars believe, may be buried somewhere in the area), and even ancient

Phoenicians seeking to civilize the land have all been offered as potentially viable candidates. But, for all of the varied theorizing, it must be admitted that the jury is most certainly still out on Avebury's *who* and *why*.

The World's Most Famous Stone Circle

As for Stonehenge, though most students of the legendary creation conclude it had its beginnings somewhere around 3100 BC, evidence of human activity in the area has been found suggesting a presence as far back as 8000 BC. And a degree of that same presence is indicative of ritualistic activity, even at that incredibly early age. But, regardless of when, precisely, large-scale construction of Stonehenge actually began, what can be said with certainty is that it is comprised of a ditch, a bank, and what are known as the Aubrey holes: round pits in the chalk that form a huge circle. And then, of course, there are those massive stone blocks.

Eighty-two of Stonehenge's so-called bluestones, some of which weigh up to 4 tons, are believed to have been transported from the Preseli Mountains in southwest Wales to the Wiltshire site, a distance of 240 miles. But the actual number of stones is in dispute, because today barely more than 40 remain. Certainly, such a mammoth operation to move such huge stones would be no easy feat in the modern era, never mind thousands of years ago. And yet, somehow, this incredible and mystifying task was successfully achieved. Stonehenge's 30 giant Sarsen stones, meanwhile, were brought from the Marlborough Downs, a distance of around 25 miles. This might sound like a much easier task than having to haul the bluestones all the way from Wales. Hardly. As noted, the Welsh stones are in the order of 4 tons. Some of the Sarsen stones from the Downs, however, weigh in at 25 tons, the heaviest around 50. And people wonder why so much mystery and intrigue surrounds the creation of Stonehenge?

Excavations at the site have uncovered the remains of cremated human bones in some of the chalk filling, which has certainly encouraged the debate about the purpose behind the construction of Stonehenge. Theories, not surprisingly, vary as widely as they do wildly, and include a place of worship, an astronomical observatory, the site of pagan ritual, an area devoted to human sacrifice, and even a spaceport for visiting extra-terrestrials. Or, maybe, a degree of all the above! The collective result of all this incredible work: the creation of one of the most iconic and recognizable ancient stone circles in the world, and one to which countless people flock and marvel at each and every year.

From King to Stone

Now we come to the somewhat less-well-known, but equally inspiring, Rollright Stones, which are situated near Long Compton, a centuries-old little village in the county of Oxfordshire. Collectively, they are comprised of a tomb, known as the Whispering Knights, a classic circle of stones called the King's Men, and a solitary stone referred to as the King's Stone. As for the time of the construction of the Rollright Stones, this appears to be a clear-cut issue: in the Neolithic and Bronze Age eras.

As with Stonehenge and Avebury, legends and abound as to the origin of the Rollright Stones. Certainly, the most engaging is that which surfaced in 1610 from a historian named William Camden. The story goes that the stones were not always stones. They originally represented an unnamed visiting king and his faithful knights, who were turned to stone, in classic Gorgon-style, one might say, by a legendary local witch, Mother Shipton. The king, not surprisingly, became the King's Stone. The bulk of his men were turned into the King's Men. A few who had initially, albeit briefly, avoided Mother Shipton's powers quickly and collectively became the Whispering Knights.

The Dancing Pillars of Merlin

It is not surprising that, taking into consideration the all-encompassing shroud of mystery that hangs over Stonehenge to this very day, a wide and varied body of fantastic legends have surfaced in relation to how the famous stone formation was made. In many respects, they closely match the tales of how levitation played a role in the construction of the pyramids of Egypt.

The world-famous Stonehenge.
(Copyright Nick Redfern.)

In the 1100s, *The History of the Kings of Britain*, penned by one Geoffrey of Monmouth, appeared, and told a wild and entertaining tale. The gist of it was that the huge stones that comprise Stonehenge actually originated in Africa and possessed magical properties that could heal the sick. According to Geoffrey, the stones were initially transported from the African continent to Ireland in the distant past by a race of mysterious giants. They ultimately made their way to Stonehenge, recorded Geoffrey, thanks to the magical skills of Merlin, the legendary occultist of King Arthur fame. Interestingly, in Geoffrey's account, each and every attempt to move the stones from their resting place in Ireland via conventional means (soldiers, ropes, and rollers) utterly failed, due, unsurprisingly, to the sheer size and weight of the stones. The only thing in Geoffrey's saga that did allow for the movement of the stones from Ireland to Stonehenge was something known as the Giants' Dance.

Although steeped in deep mystery, the Giants' Dance was said to be an ancient ritual in which, if one knew the magical ways of the wizards of old (prized secrets of an early, mystery-shrouded era that Merlin was said to possess and carefully guard), one could move the massive stones with relative ease. Rather intriguingly, the Giants' Dance relied on the use of so-called magical music to shift the huge pillars.

The idea that the huge stones of Stonehenge had their origins in Africa, then Ireland, before finally being brought to Wiltshire, England, is not just unlikely. It's demonstrably not true. But, one cannot rule out the possibility that if fragmentary and distorted old tales of advanced, acoustic technology playing a decisive role in the construction of Stonehenge had been passed down from generation to generation, this may well go some way toward explaining how, and under what circumstances, the story as told by Geoffrey of Monmouth came to develop an undetermined number of centuries after the construction of possibly the world's most famous stone circle began.

Healing Stones

It's worth recalling that the legends uncovered by Geoffrey of Monmouth suggested the giant stones of Stonehenge, possibly maneuvered by acoustics, possessed healing properties. Interestingly, a great deal of research has been undertaken in recent years into the effects of acoustics on the human body. For example, the Website of the Encinitas, California–based Center for Neuroacoustic Research notes: "Cutting edge, scientific sound technology, combined with a deep understanding of the ancient use of sound to heal and expand consciousness, has brought CNR the ability to balance the autonomic nervous system in real time" (Jo Thompson, 2011).

And then there is the exact opposite: namely, the negative aspects of acoustic technology on the human body. A formerly secret Defense Intelligence Agency (DIA) document of 1972 deals with certain effects of ultrasounds on human beings—effects that led to drowsiness and an abnormal need for sleep. Experiments undertaken by the DIA using directed acoustic weaponry revealed that some individuals even fell asleep while standing up. More alarming, the files state that, as far back as the 1960s, the Department of Defense had been carefully researching the possibility of utilizing both high- and low-frequency sound waves as a means of inducing heart attacks in otherwise-healthy people.

Is it perhaps possible, then, that the ancients knew as much about the effects of acoustics on the human body as they did on the movement of gigantic stones? Taking into consideration the research of the Center for Neuroacoustic Research, and the Defense Intelligence Agency, perhaps the old legends surrounding Stonehenge and its healing qualities are not just the stuff of myth and folklore after all.

It's also important to note the words of Paul Devereux, an expert in the field of ancient sites and stone circles in Britain and elsewhere, who said: "Archaeologists have finally realized that ancient people had ears, and have discovered that various kinds of acoustic effects—from eerie echoes to resonant frequencies that can affect the brain—seem to have been an intentionally planned component of a number of prehistoric sites worldwide, from ruined temples to rock art locations" (Devereux, 2011).

And, in just the same way that the great stones of Stonehenge were said to have been maneuvered into place via magical means, similar legends are attached to numerous other British-based stone circles. The Cock-Crow Stone at Looe, Cornwall, England, for example, is said to turn around three times when a cock crows in its vicinity. Likewise, there is a legend suggesting the Whetstone in the English county of Hertfordshire has been seen to walk to the edges of the River Wye. And a similar tale is attached to Avebury's heavyweight, the Swindon Stone: At the witching-hour, rather appropriately, it begins to move of its own accord by first swiveling on its axis and then, shrouded in darkness, moving around the old roads of Avebury.

Of course, we should not interpret, or accept, these tales literally. But one thing they all have in common is an overriding belief that, in times long past, the stones, which still comprise ancient stone circles and historic sites in the UK, had the ability to move via magical or supernatural means. Did such tales represent mere folklore, or were they really distorted accounts of a lost and forgotten technology used by the ancients? Were those secrets then passed down through numerous generations and ultimately became distorted, bit by bit, until they became the stuff of nothing more than legend and campfire tales? Taking into consideration the fact that very similar accounts surfaced from Egypt, Boeotia, and Uxmal, a solid argument can be made that these widespread accounts had at least some basis in reality, even if the science involved eventually became exaggerated and distorted by folklore, myth, and the passage of the centuries.

And, it seems, elements of the British Ministry of Defense has taken an interest in these very issues, too.

STONEHENGE AND SECRET FILES

The Plasma Project

In May 2006, it was announced that, after decades of secretly investigating UFOs, the British Ministry of Defense had come to the conclusion that aliens were *not* visiting the United Kingdom. The MoD's claims were revealed within the pages of a formerly classified document titled *Unidentified Aerial Phenomena in the UK Air Defence Region*, and code-named *Project Condign*, which had been commissioned in 1996 and was completed by February 2000. Released under the terms of the Freedom of Information Act thanks specifically to the work of Dr. David Clarke, who has a PhD in Folklore, and UFO researcher Gary Anthony, the

465-page document demonstrates how air defense experts had concluded that UFO sightings were probably the result of natural, but quite rare phenomena, such as ball lightning and atmospheric plasmas. Some UFOs, wrote the still-unknown author of the MoD's report, may have been unusual, but they were not of any particular defense significance.

Inevitably, many UFO investigators claimed that the MoD's report was merely a ruse to hide its secret knowledge of alien encounters, crashed UFOs, and high-level *X-Files*-type conspiracies. Although the government firmly denied such claims, the report did reveal a number of significant conclusions of a genuinely intriguing nature. The atmospheric plasmas, which were believed to be the cause of so many UFO reports, were not fully understood, said the MoD, and the magnetic and electric fields that emanated from plasmas could adversely affect the human nervous system. And that was not all. Clarke and Anthony revealed that, "Volume 3 of the report refers to research and studies carried out in a number of foreign nations into UAPs [Unidentified Aerial Phenomena], atmospheric plasmas, and their potential military applications" (Clarke, 2006).

Even more remarkable, a number of MoD reports of unusual plasmas having notable effects on the human mind and body—and possibly even possessing the ability to induce hallucinatory states—emanated from Avebury and Stonehenge. They were investigated by an elite arm of the Royal Air Force that, for years, had its headquarters at a strategic military base called Royal Air Force Rudloe Manor.

A Secret Base

Situated within the green and pleasant countryside of Wiltshire, England, less than 30 miles from Stonehenge and only 17 miles from Avebury, Royal Air Force (RAF) Rudloe Manor has for decades been the subject of numerous stories concerning clandestine UFO studies undertaken by British authorities. The powers-that-be assert the stories are utter nonsense and represent little more than modern-day folklore. Meanwhile, others maintain that several crashed UFOs and an untold number of alien bodies are stored deep below Rudloe Manor, within the mass of tunnels and caverns that undoubtedly exist under the base and throughout the surrounding area. Determining where the tales end and truth begins is somewhat problematic. But one thing can be said with certainty: This area of Wiltshire is the source of what is known as Bath stone, which has been quarried for centuries, hence the existence of the huge underground openings from where the stone was extracted.

Until 1998, the duties of Rudloe Manor's Provost and Security Services (P&SS) included the investigation of crime and disciplinary matters involving RAF personnel, security vetting of personnel, and the issuing of identity cards, passes, and permits. Far more significant, investigators attached to the P&SS are also trained in the field of counter-intelligence (C/I). Such training is undertaken at the RAF Police School. Prospective candidates for counter-intelligence work are required to take specialized courses in subjects such as computer security and surveillance. Before being considered for C/I work, personnel have to attain the rank of corporal within the RAF Police. C/I investigators are responsible for issues affecting the security of the RAF, which includes the loss and theft of classified documents, matters pertaining to espionage cases, and the protection of royalty and VIPs when visiting RAF stations.

Also situated with the headquarters of the P&SS is a division known as the Flying Complaints Flight, which primarily investigates complaints of low-flying military aircraft in Britain. UFO researcher Timothy Good has related the account of a former special investigator with the P&SS who claimed specific knowledge of its involvement in the UFO subject. "I am sure beyond any reasonable shadow of doubt," Good's source told him, "that all initial investigations into UFOs are carried out by investigators of the P&SS who are serving in a small secret unit with the Flying Complaints Flight based at HQ, P&SS, Rudloe Manor" (Good, 1991).

Despite the fact that Good's source wished to remain anonymous, mine were quite open with their identities. Jonathan Turner served with the Royal Air Force for 10 years as a medic and retired in 1993. While stationed at RAF Lyneham, Turner learned that reports of UFO sightings by military pilots were never recorded in the flight logs. Instead, details would first be channelled through to the squadron commander, who would then advise the station commander of the situation. From there, all relevant information would be forwarded to the P&SS for examination. Similarly, Neil Rusling, no less a source than the treasurer of the Royal Air Force Police Association, told me an illuminating story. In December 1996 I learned directly from Rusling that he had served with the RAF's counter-intelligence section. He told me with absolute certainty that the P&SS's Flying Complaints Flight was involved in UFO studies.

But it was not just UFO researchers that were picking up on tales of clandestine activities being undertaken at Rudloe Manor. On October 17, 1996, the late Member of the British Parliament Martin Redmond asked a number of UFO-related questions in Parliament and touched upon the stories relating to Rudloe. Eleven days later he was informed, in part, that there existed at Rudloe several departments with intriguing backgrounds and duties, including the Detachment of 1001 Signals Unit, which operated the British military communications satellite system; No. 1 Signals Unit, which provided voice and data communications for the RAF, Royal Navy, Army, and Ministry of Defense; and the Controller Defense Communications Network, a tri-service unit controlling worldwide communications for the military. The DCN was situated 120 feet underground and was capable of housing no fewer than 55,000 people in the event of a national emergency.

The real coup, however, came when I located a file at the Public Record Office at Kew that conclusively proved that the stories of clandestine UFO investigations undertaken by the P&SS were true and dated back to at least 1962. And one file in particular, discussed at length in my book *The Real Men in Black*, suggested that some of the so-called MIB reports in the United Kingdom could be traced back directly to the activities of the P&SS's Special Investigation Section. Something secret of a UFO nature was definitely going on at Rudloe, and perhaps deep below it, too. But that is not all. It's now time to take a look at what the P&SS has learned about the strange secrets of Avebury and Stonehenge.

The Monster of the Stones

According to a now-declassified, six-page file titled "'Unexplained Event' at Avebury, Wilts.," that had been prepared by a P&SS officer, an extraordinary event of near-monstrous proportions occurred within the old stones of

Avebury on a September day in 1962. Early on the morning in question, a hysterical telephone call was received at RAF Melksham, situated only approximately 15 miles from Avebury. The caller claimed to have seen a UFO hovering in the vicinity of the ancient standing stones at Avebury on the previous night and demanded that the military send someone to speak with her immediately.

The files report that the witness, whose name is excised from the declassified files, was a "middle-aged spinster" who had lived in Avebury all of her adult life and who was fascinated by archaeological history. She told the investigating officer she often strolled around the stones at night, marvelling at their creation and musing upon their history. On the previous evening, while amid the stones, she was both startled and amazed to see a small ball of light, perhaps 2 feet in diameter, gliding slowly toward her. It was a plasma-like globe, very much like the type studied decades later by the brains behind the Ministry of Defense's *Project Condign* report.

Transfixed and rooted to the spot, the woman watched as the plasma ball closed in on her at a height of about 12 feet. The ball then stopped around 15 feet from her (horizontally), as small amounts of what looked like liquid metal slowly and silently dripped from it to the ground. Then, in an instant, the ball exploded in a bright, white flash. For a moment the witness was blinded by its intensity, and she instinctively fell to her knees. When her eyes cleared, however, she was faced with a horrific sight. The ball of light had gone, but on the ground in front of her was what she could only describe as a monstrous, writhing worm. The creature, said the woman, was about 5 feet long, perhaps 8 or 9 inches thick, and its skin was milk-white in color. As she slowly rose to her feet, the creature's head turned suddenly in her direction and two bulging eyes opened. When it began to move unsteadily toward the woman in a caterpillar-like fashion, she emitted a hysterical scream and fled the scene.

Rushing back home, she slammed the door shut. The files reflect the witness had practically barricaded herself in her home, was almost incoherent with fear, and agreed to return to the scene only after lengthy coaxing. After assuring the woman that her case would be taken very seriously and requesting that she discuss the events with no one, the officer headed back to RAF Melksham. A classified report was duly prepared and dispatched up the chain of command. For more than a week, plainclothes military personnel secretly wandered casually among the stones seeking evidence of anything unusual. Nothing, evidence-wise, was ever found.

Notably, however, the conclusion of the investigating officer reads as follows: "Miss [Deleted] experienced something foreign to her normal surroundings. Whatever it may have been is beyond Royal Air Force investigators. It has the suggestion of flying saucers, and Miss [Deleted] admitted as much." In joking style, the officer closed his report with the following words: "For the worm, perhaps the Loch Ness Monster has moved house!" (Provost & Security Services, 1962).

But not everyone was laughing.

Secret Studies of Stone

A copy of the Avebury report was sent to AI5b, an Air Intelligence office of the British Air Ministry at Whitehall, London. In a handwritten memo, one of its staff members noted to P&SS HQ: "We concur with the flying saucer comparisons. A.I. has a policy of not commenting publicly on our interest because of the inevitable accusations about 'hiding the truth about flying saucers' that flying saucer sleuths will make if A.I. interest becomes public knowledge. We have never found a shred of information that we have cousins in the universe. But A.I. is interested in sighting occurrences where the reporter's event may have caused changes in eyesight/vision and hallucinations and audible events which Miss [Deleted] seems [deleted]. A.I. requests any similar reports to the Miss [Deleted] statement be forwarded to this office" (AI5b, 1962).

The British Ministry of Defense has secretly investigated the mysteries of Avebury, Stonehenge, and the Rollright Stones. (Copyright Nick Redfern.)

Further exchanges between AI5b and the P&SS revealed something even more significant: An element of the British Army had quietly investigated a number of reports of similar balls of light seen, in 1958 and 1959, in and around Stonehenge. And, in these cases, those affected were military personnel. Salisbury Plain is a huge expanse of land (it covers no less than 300 square miles) in the county of Wiltshire, which people have called home since Neolithic times. In fact, Stonehenge itself stands within the confines of this very plain. But there is far more to Salisbury Plain than Stonehenge. Since the latter part of the 19th century, the British military has used the vast expanse of land for training purposes. And, today, the Ministry of Defense owns 150 square miles of Salisbury Plain, almost 40 square miles of which are permanently out of bounds to the British people.

According to government files, on seven occasions between March 1958 and August 1959, military personnel engaged in training exercises on Salisbury Plain reported seeing (always late at night or in the early hours of the morning) strange aerial balls of light, somewhere in the order of size of a basketball, hovering above them at heights that varied wildly from several hundred feet to perhaps only 40 or 50 feet. On four of such occasions, the balls of light were carefully pursued—under strict orders from senior officers not to approach them too closely—to none other than Stonehenge, where they stopped, hovered in mid-air for a few moments over the huge stones, and then soared away into the night sky.

Most disturbing of all, on a couple of the occasions, excitement got the better of some of the younger trainees, who decided to try to get a closer look at the strange plasma-like phenomena, particularly when the phenomena came close to the ground. Each and every one of the personnel who encountered the plasmas up close and personal reported very much the same thing:

a hallucinatory experience of fantastic proportions. One saw the ball of light mutate into the form of what resembled a dragon of classic mythology. For another, it was an angel that appeared. A third described seeing the Virgin Mary (recall Marian visions were addressed by RAND's Jean M. Hungerford in classified U.S. documentation of 1950). And a fourth claimed to have encountered an octopus-like creature that looked like it had oozed straight out of the pages of an H.P. Lovecraft novel. But, those troops who kept their distance could only see their comrades standing utterly still, staring at the balls of light as if transfixed or hypnotized via some strange, unearthly power that had the ability to alter their perceptions of what they were really seeing, which may very well have been precisely what was happening.

Moreover, the files demonstrate that these particular encounters provoked a great deal of concern on the part of the British military's highest echelons, to the extent that a small project was established to address the strange experiences. Oddly enough, however, we have only the very briefest of data on this affair because as internal MoD memoranda of 1978 notes: "To our cost we are relying on institutional memory—searches have failed to locate the record we are told was preserved" (Defense Intelligence Staff, 1978).

Visions and the MoD

Although the crucial documentation generated as a result of the British military's experiences at Stonehenge in 1958 and 1959 is curiously missing, it does not take a genius to understand why the British Army, Air Intelligence and, in later years, Defense Intelligence Staff, were so deeply interested in these particular reports. The reason was spelled out officially and secretly in a report from March 1978 that summarized the late-1950s events for elements of the MoD's Defense Intelligence Staff that were involved in the development of new and alternative forms of weaponry in the late 1970s and ultimately through to the early 1980s.

Stonehenge: a place of visionary encounters. (Copyright Nick Redfern.)

The author of the report (whose name has been blacked-out on available files) wrote: "...men closest to the phenom-enon reported 'visions' of many types—audible and visual. Inasmuch as each 'vision' was unique to each witness our conclusion is the phenomenon affects parts of the brain categorised by [two-lines deleted]. Reproducing these ef-fects has an obvious potential for military application and D/I research. These are challenging areas the Soviet Bloc has explored since the 1960s" (Ibid).

Notably, the writer of the DIS document added the following handwritten note at the foot of the document: "Much as we would prefer not to follow this road there is the connection between the 1958 and 1959 reports and UK monuments (Stonehenge, Rollright). I can see we may al-ready have some problems convincing [deleted] to provide funding for [deleted] without having to bring 'Chariots of the Gods' into the equation. Then there are the comments contained in the Rollright reports of phenomena being 'alive'. All this needs to be studied in some detail—funding, as usual, permitting" (Ibid.).

This particular section of the document is as frustrat-ingly brief as it is highly illuminating. First, it demon-strates that two decades after the events in and around Stonehenge, the Ministry of Defense was planning on re-addressing those old cases, with a view to trying to deter-mine if the phenomena could be harnessed and utilized on the battlefield. Second, that the DIS planned to try to secure funding to address the links between mind-altering plasmas and ancient sites is truly extraordinary. Third, is the refer-ence to plasma phenomena being alive. Finally, there is the brief reference to so-called vision experiences at Rollright.

A Rollright Monster

In 1977, the aforementioned Paul Devereux established what became titled the *Dragon Project*, the purpose of which was to study claims that certain British prehistoric sites had unusual forces or energies attached to them, including magnetic, infrared, and ultrasonic anomalies. While investigating none other than the Rollright Stones, Devereux reported that one of the team members, described as being a well-known archaeologist, was sitting in a van when a large, unidentified, lumbering, hair-covered beast walked by. An instant later, it vanished.

Could this sighting of what the witness perceived to be an immense, unknown creature actually have been generated by plasma-style phenomena present at the old stones? That the British Ministry of Defense's DIS apparently had on file earlier, vision-based experiences from within the Rollright Stones makes this particular possibility an altogether distinctly sound one. But, if such plasmas as those described *can* induce visionary states, how, precisely, are they achieved? A few researchers think they might have the answer. But, just before we get to those same researchers, there are two final observations worth noting regarding the Rollright Stones.

Another event of a curious nature at the Rollright Stones was reported by Murry Hope, the author of many books, including *Practical Egyptian Magic*, *Ancient Egypt: The Sirius Connection*, and *Atlantis: Myth or Reality?* Hope noted, after a visit to the stones, they seemed to be "programmed to respond to (or resonate with) a specific sonic, which had nothing to do with time as we know it. The original program must have been inserted either by an advanced race from the far past whose knowledge of sonics far exceeded the bounds of present-day science, or from some extraterrestrial source." Hope ultimately accepted the former as being the most likely option of the two (Richardson, 2001).

Second, an interesting legend is attached to the Rollright Stones that echoes right back to the story of Abu al-Hasan Ali al-Mas'udi, and those of the ancient Greeks and the Phoenicians in relation to huge stones moved by the power of the Gods, ancient ritual, or acoustic technology. It is said that on occasion the Rollright Stones have been seen to come alive—at midnight, no less—and perform strange dances in the immediate vicinity. Or move via the means of a lost technology. Now, back to those visions.

Playful Curiosity

Dr. David Clarke and Gary Anthony noted the following in relation to the secret study of the Ministry of Defense called *Project Condign*: "Mr. X [the title given by Clarke and Anthony to the still-unidentified MoD-sponsored author] goes even further by drawing upon the controversial research and conclusions of research carried out at Laurentian University by Michael Persinger" (Clarke, 2006).

Dr. Greg Little, commenting on Persinger's work, says: "Persinger's research indicates that people who come into close contact with these charged plasma forms experience altered states of consciousness producing a host of strange visions: UFO abductions, apparitional phenomena, sightings of improbable creatures (e.g., Bigfoot), fairies, and alien-like creatures" (Little, 2003).

What, exactly, is the temporal lobe that Persinger believes may play a significant role in such matters? Essentially, it is a region of the cerebral cortex that is found beneath the Sylvian fissure on both the left and right hemispheres of the brain, which is involved in auditory processing. In addition, the temporal lobe plays an important role in the processing of semantics in both speech and vision, as well as in the formation of long-term memory and its transference from the short-term memory state. In other words, the temporal lobe is a vital component of the process by which we interpret and compartmentalize audio-visual phenomena, and plays a significant role in the way in which we recall such phenomena, via our memories.

Phenomena having the ability to influence, or outright manipulate, such a complex tool as the temporal lobe might very well possess the ability to make us see, hear, and later recall just about anything they wanted us to. This may have included such fantastic things reported by elements of the British Army near Stonehenge in the 1950s (including the Virgin Mary, an angel, a dragon, and a monstrous, octopus-type beast), the large worm-like animal at Avebury in the early 1960s, and the hairy beast at the Rollright Stones in the 1970s, as described by Paul Devereux.

Devereux says that a not-fully understood byproduct of stresses and strains in the Earth's crust may indeed produce such plasmas; however, in other instances, he offers that there is an intriguing possibility these plasmas may very well represent literal life forms. Devereux notes that if such reports can be considered credible, then at least some of the lights may be demonstrating a "playful, animal-like curiosity" (Devereux, 2011).

Expanding on this issue, Devereux adds that this "raises the tricky question of the nature of consciousness.... To even suggest that consciousness might manifest in geo-physical contexts as well as biological ones is to go beyond the pale"—not, it seems, for the Ministry of Defense's DIS of 1978, however, who were looking to secure sufficient funding to research this very area of the mysterious plasmas at Rollright displaying evidence of a certain degree of sentience (Ibid.).

This leaves one critically important question unanswered: Why did all of the experiences (Stonehenge in the 1950s, Avebury in 1962, and the site of the Rollright Stones,) at one time known only to officialdom, occur at ancient, historic locations and formations? That is a question that remains unknown. Or, perhaps more correctly, it remains unknown outside of the vaults of the British Ministry of Defense. It seems fair to conclude, though, that there are those within the government of the United Kingdom who possess an awareness of something as astonishing as it is disturbing: Ancient stone circles are home to, or seem to attract, extraordinary phenomena that possess the ability to significantly manipulate human perception.

PAST, PRESENT, AND FUTURE

Having now carefully digested a wealth of truly extraordinary data relative to official interest in the many and varied mysteries of the ancient past, is there anything that can be said with a firm degree of certainty with respect to what has prompted such deep, unending interest? Let's take a look.

Clearly it makes no sense at all for the world of government to have spent (and to continue to spend) countless years, manpower, and dollars researching the history and actions of long-gone civilizations that held sway millennia ago, just for the sheer hell of it. There has to have been a significant motivation in trying to understand the full story of Noah's Ark, the construction of the pyramids, the nature

251

of Djinns, the claims of connections between early civilizations and so-called ancient astronauts, the mystery of England's Stonehenge, the Dead Sea Scrolls, and much more.
So, what was the specific nature of that motivation?

Regarding the saga of Noah's Ark, we have seen evidence
that it was studied by (among many others in government)
staff attached to a secret military operation code-named
Project Moon Dust. The purpose of Moon Dust was to secure advanced technologies of new and novel natures that
could aid in furthering America's military arsenal, as well as
the government's scientific and technological capabilities.

In relation to its quest to understand, and potentially
even interact with, Middle Eastern Djinns, as outlined by
Philip Imbrogno, the motivation was very similar, if not
downright identical. It was to harness, for U.S. military
gain, the extraordinary psychic powers and dimension-
hopping skills that these creatures reportedly possess.

Much the same can be said for the official interest provoked by the theories and conclusions of the late Dr. Morris
K. Jessup and Bruce Cathie, namely that in the distant past
there existed astonishing technologies that, today, we would
place under the headings of "Anti-Gravity" and "levitation."

Moving away from the United States, the British Ministry
of Defense's research into vision-style experiences at Stonehenge was prompted by the possibility of using such intriguing, but not fully comprehended, technology on the battlefield.
And Adolf Hitler wished dearly to create an arsenal comprised
of all-powerful, ancient, religious artifacts that he could unleash upon the Allies at the height of World War II.

The message that this spells out to us is very clear and
wholly undeniable, and it gets right to the heart of what has
commanded this extensive Pentagon-driven journey into

the past: Governments have been seeking to do nothing less than exploit and weaponize what they perceive as being the powers of the gods, the lost sciences of whole races of people long-gone, and the awesome and devastating might of ancient astronauts from worlds far away. After all, why else would governments take an interest in puzzles of the past? To further our knowledge of archaeology? Hardly! Using the past to create more and more weapons in the present and the future makes perfect, but most regrettable, sense.

Because the average man, woman, or child does not have access to anti-gravity technology, to devices that allow for maneuvering between dimensions, or to any of the other miracle-like technologies of distant eras described in this book, then we can surmise one of two things: (a) that governments have indeed replicated the secret technologies of the ancients, but prefer to keep them out of the hands of the public, locked behind closed doors, and ready and waiting for the day when they may be needed on the battlefield; or (b) that despite all the digging, the research, and the careful scrutiny of ancient manuscripts, governments are still very much scratching the surface when it comes to harnessing the exact nature of the people and their attendant technologies that blossomed and ultimately fell long before ours.

We can never rule out the first scenario, and indeed it would be logical for military agencies to keep hidden any real and radical advances made in the fields of anti-gravity, levitation, and more. The fear of the enemy, or of a potential enemy, developing their own equivalents of such technology if it was placed onto the open market would alone be very good reason to classify all such findings and developments under a top-secret banner.

As far as the second scenario is concerned, maybe we sometimes give our governments too much credit. From studying those cases where there has been clear interest exhibited in a wide body of ancient mysteries, one almost gets the idea that, though governments suspect a great deal and are very intrigued by the nature of the people that preceded us, maybe they don't know much more than those of us who are on the outside looking in. Certainly agencies of officialdom have secured a lot of extraordinary data on what sound like incredibly advanced, ancient sciences that easily eclipsed anything of the modern era. They suspect atomic weapons may have been used in localized skirmishes thousands of years ago. They note, with distinct uneasiness, the Mars-Egypt connections. And they have clearly addressed the mysteries of how the pyramids were constructed. But maybe that's where things come to a sudden end—with a lot of data, numerous suspicions, but no hard evidence, and just frustrating bafflement due to the extraordinarily long passage of time, and the old secrets they so yearn to uncover having been lost, hidden, or destroyed, possibly thousands of years ago.

There is, however, a third scenario. It's one that allows for both of the previous scenarios to have some validity and merit to them, but it also offers another reason behind the undeniable secrecy and obfuscation surrounding such matters. A side effect of governmental digging into the past may well be a realization that history, as we perceive it today, is manifestly inaccurate to a massive degree. Maybe governments have all the answers to what came before us, possibly they have some of the answers, or perhaps they have just a very few, albeit along with a lot of theories and ideas. But what the history of the Pentagon's penetration of the past may tell us is that the history books need to be rewritten. Some might argue that the government's findings suggest the very nature of religion itself might need to be readdressed.

Whether a person is a true believer, an agnostic, or an atheist, none can deny that religion has spiritually elevated people, unified whole races, and given comfort to billions in times of need. But, religion has also been the cause of war, destruction, and death on a very large scale. It is one of the absolute cornerstones of human culture. From what we have seen in this book, it could be argued that many of the Pentagon's discoveries suggest those same religious cornerstones may not have been founded by gods (or by *a* God), but by aliens from afar or by very early human cultures that stumbled upon, and duly harnessed, amazing technologies that still largely elude us to this day, and that were interpreted as the work of deities.

The reason why so much secrecy surrounds what the Pentagon knows about the pyramids, about Vimanas, and about numerous other ancient marvels may not be because of the alternative technologies employed in their collective construction. The secrecy may result from something else: Should governments one day come clean on their knowledge of the formative years of human civilization, that action may very well require a total rewriting of just about each and every worldwide religion. One can scarcely begin to imagine the chaos that would erupt, worldwide, if an announcement was made that all faiths—Christianity, Islam, Buddhism, Hinduism, the list goes on—were based on distorted tales of visitations from the extraterrestrial equivalents of NASA's *Apollo* astronauts.

Similarly, if the Pentagon believes that the remarkable stone creations of the past were the work of very terrestrial (as opposed to extra-terrestrial) people who destroyed themselves in atomic infernos, an official revelation of such a theory might also lead to chaos and disruption. If we are shown evidence that numerous societies and cultures surfaced long before our own, all of whom destroyed themselves one by one, and became nothing more than the stuff of legends and tales, this would surely lead many of us to wonder how long it would be before we, too, inevitably followed suit. A planetary attitude of depression and despondency might very well spread with disturbing speed. Of course, these scenarios should be seen for the speculation they surely are. Until the government actually places all its cards on the table, we'll never really know.

We started this book with one movie—*Raiders of the Lost Ark*—and we will finish it with another. In the closing minutes of the 1968 movie *Planet of the Apes*, Charlton Heston's character, an astronaut named Taylor, heads off to a mysterious desert area of the nightmarish, ape-ruled world into which he has been plunged. It is a dark and terrifying realm known to the apes as the Forbidden Zone. Taylor does not realize it, but, rather than having traveled across space, he has actually been on a journey through time. Taylor is not on a faraway world at all. Instead, he is right here, on Earth, but millennia in the future, at a time when the human race has been reduced to primitive state, and powerful, iron-fisted apes with the ability to speak run the planet.

What Taylor also does not yet know is that deep within the Forbidden Zone are the last few radioactive remnants of our long-gone civilization—including a half-buried and scarred Statue of Liberty—which was destroyed thousands of years earlier during an all-out atomic exchange with the Soviets. As he heads off in search of the answers, Taylor is warned by Dr. Zaius—the apes' minister of science—that, with respect to the distant past and humankind's forgotten and lost history, "You may not like what you find."

Perhaps, just like Taylor, who ultimately learns the shocking truth of how and why his culture and world were destroyed so long ago, the Pentagon has also found something shocking about the ancient past that not a single one of *us* will like.

BIBLIOGRAPHY

*All websites were last reviewed in December 2011.

"Acoustic Levitation." *http://videos.mitrasites.com/acoustic-levitation. html*, 2011.

AI5b Memorandum. *Reports on Aerial Phenomena*, September 28, 1962.

Al-Ashqar, Umar Sulaiman. *The World of the Jinn and Devils*. Boulder, Colo: Al Basheer Company, 1998.

Albarelli, Jr., H.P. *A Terrible Mistake*. Walterville, Ore.: Trine Day, 2009.

Alford, Alan F. "The Mystery of the Stones at Baalbek." *www.world mysteries.com/mpl_5b1.htm*, 2009.

Alleged Assassination Plots Involving Foreign Leaders, Interim Report of the Select Committee to Study Government Operations with Respect to Intelligence Activities. Washington, D.C.: U.S. Government Printing Office, 1975.

Allen, Thomas George. *Horus in the Pyramid Texts*. Chicago, Ill.: University of Chicago Libraries, 1916.

Al-Mas-udi, Abu al-Hasan Ali. *Meadows of Gold and Mines of Gems*. (Trans. Paul Lunde and Caroline Stone.) London: Kegan Paul International, 1989.

Alouf, Michael M. *History of Baalbek*. Boston, Mass.: American Press, 1944.

"Aluka." The Demoniacal. *http://thedemoniacal.blogspot.com/2010/ 07/aluka.html*, July 7, 2010.

Anderson, Floyd. "Jim Marrs Lecture—Ancient Technology from the Past: White Powder Gold." *http://floydanderson.blogspot.com/2007/05/jim-marrs-lecture-ancient-technology.html*, May 5, 2007.

Anderson, Ken. *Hitler and the Occult*. New York: Prometheus Books, 1995.

"Anti-gravity Booming." *Aero Digest*, March 1956.

"Anunaki." *www.hiddencodes.com/annunaki.htm*, 2011.

"The Anunaki, Ancient Gods." *www.zetatalk.com/index/blog0926.htm*, 2011.

Arnold, Kenneth, statement to the Federal Bureau of Investigation (FBI), Washington D.C., June 28, 1947.

"Avebury: A Present from the Past." *www.avebury-web.co.uk/*, 2011.

"Baalbek Stone of the Pregnant Woman." *http://atheism.about.com/od/religiousplaces/ig/Baalbek-Temples-Lebanon/Baalbek-Stone-Pregnant-Woman.htm*, 2011.

Badrinath, Chaturvedi. *The Mahabharata*. New Delhi, India: Orient Longman, 2006.

Bahn, Paul G. *Lost Cities*. New York: Welcome Rain, 1999.

Baigent, Michael. *The Jesus Scrolls*. London: Harper, 2007.

Baigent, Michael, and Richard Leigh. *The Dead Sea Scrolls Deception*. London: Simon & Schuster, 1993.

Baigent, Michael, Richard Leigh, and Henry Lincoln. *Holy Blood, Holy Grail*. New York: Dell Publishing, 1983.

Bailey, Regina. "Temporal Lobes." *http://biology.about.com/od/anatomy/p/temporal-lobes.htm*, 2011.

Bamford James. *The Puzzle Palace*. London: Sidgwick & Jackson, 1983.

Barber, Richard. *The Holy Grail: Imagination and Belief*. Cambridge, Mass.: Harvard University Press, 2004.

Battles, Dominique. *The Medieval Tradition of Thebes*. New York: Routledge, 2004.

Berendt, H.C. "Dr. Puharich and Uri Geller." *Journal of the Society for Psychical Research, Vol. 48, No. 768*, June 1976.

Berlitz, Charles. *The Lost Ship of Noah*. New York: Fawcett Crest, 1987.

Berlitz, Charles, and William L. Moore. *The Philadelphia Experiment*. London: Panther Books, 1980.

———. *The Roswell Incident*. London: Panther Books, 1980.

Binder, Eando. *Puzzle of the Space Pyramids*. New York: Curtis Books, 1971.

Binder, Otto O. *Victory in Space*. New York: Walker, 1962.

"Birthplace of America's Missile and Space Activity." *www.nasa.gov/ pdf/449089main_White_Sands_Missile_Range_Fact_Sheet.pdf*, 2011.

Blank, Wayne. "Bread of the Presence." *www.keyway.ca/ htm2004/20040824.htm*, August 24, 2004.

Boeche, Raymond W. *Caught in a Web of Deception*. Lincoln, Nebr.: University of Nebraska Press, 1994.

Bogdanos, Matthew, with William Patrick. *Thieves of Baghdad*. New York: Bloomsbury, 2005.

Bollinger, B. "Vrykolakas: The Bloodless Vampire." *www.ufodigest.com/ news/0209/vrykolakas.php*, February 20, 2009.

Brandenberg, John, and Monica Rix Paxson. *Dead Mars, Dying Earth*. Berkeley, Calif.: Crossing Press, 2000.

Brennan, Herbie. *Martian Genesis*. New York: Dell Publishing, 2000.

Brier, Bob, and Jean-Pierre Houdin. *The Secret of the Great Pyramid*. New York: Harper Paperbacks, 2009.

Bruce, Alexandra. *The Philadelphia Experiment Murder*. New York: Sky Books, 2001.

Burger, Richard, and Lucy Salazar (editors). *Machu Picchu: Unveiling the Mystery of the Incas*. New Haven, Conn.: Yale University Press, 2004.

Burl, Aubrey. *A Guide to the Stone Circles of Britain, Ireland and Brittany*. New Haven, Conn.: Yale University Press, 2005.

Callimahos, Lambros D. *The Harmonic Theory of Cathie, Bruce*. National Security Agency, June 3, 1972.

Cameron, Grant. "President John F. Kennedy." *www.presidentialufo. com/john-f-kennedy/72-president-john-f-kennedy*, August 1, 2009.

Campbell, Roland. *Noah's Ark: Select Rumours from the Front*. Secret Intelligence Service, November 28, 1948.

Cantwheel, Thomas. Letter to Timothy Cooper, February 29, 1996.

Carew, Mairead. *Tara and the Ark of the Covenant*. Dublin, Ireland: Royal Irish Academy, 2003.

Carlotto, Mark J. *The Martian Enigmas*. Berkeley, Calif.: North Atlantic Books, 1991.

Carney, Scott. "Did a Comet Cause the Great Flood?" *Discover Magazine*, November 2007.

Cassidy, David. *J. Robert Oppenheimer and the American Century*. New York: Pi Press, 2005.

Cathie, Bruce. *The Energy Grid: Harmonic 695*. Kempton, Ill.: Adventures Unlimited Press, 1997.

———. *The Harmonic Conquest of Space*. Kempton, Ill.: Adventures Unlimited Press, 1998.

Cayce, Edgar, and Hugh Lynn Cayce (editor). *Edgar Cayce on Atlantis*. New York: Paperback Library, 1968.

Central Intelligence Agency. Memorandum, February 7, 1994.

———. Memorandum, January 21, 1993.

———. "Noah's Ark 1974-1982." *www.foia.cia.gov/docs/DOC_0000728028/DOC_0000728028.pdf*. Note: This link is to a CIA-originated summary of the documentation the Agency has declassified on Noah's Ark via the terms of the Freedom of Information Act. The full documentation cited in this book, and from which the summary was derived, has not yet been posted on-line by the CIA, but is available via the FOIA.

Child, James R. *The Voynich Manuscript Revisited*. National Security Agency (undated). The document can be downloaded at the National Security Agency's Website at this link: *www.nsa.gov/applications/search/index.cfm?q=Voynich*.

Childress, David Hatcher. *Vimana Aircraft of Ancient India & Atlantis*. Kempton, Ill.: Adventures Unlimited Press. 1995.

Chippindale, Christopher. *Stonehenge Complete*. London: Thames & Hudson, 2004.

"The CIA, Andrija Puharich, & the Council of Nine." *www.worldenlightenment.com/The-Order-of-Things/CIA-Andrija-Puharich-Council-of-Nine.htm*, 2011.

Clark, Ronald W. *The Man Who Broke Purple: The Life of Colonel William F. Friedman, Who Deciphered the Japanese Code in World War II*. New York: Little Brown & Co, 1977.

Clarke, Dr. David, and Gary Anthony. "The British MoD Study: Project Condign." *International UFO Reporter*, Vol. 30, No. 4, 2006.

Cleaver, A. V. "'Electro-Gravitics': What it Is—or Might Be." *Journal of the British Interplanetary Society*, April–June, 1957.

"Clooney Plans Movie About Fake Movie." *www.mania.com/clooney-plans-movie-about- fake-movie_article_54561.html*, May 3, 2007.

Coe, Michael D., and Rex Koontz. *Mexico: From the Olmecs to the Aztecs*. New York: Thames & Hudson, 2002.

Collins, Andrew. *Beneath the Pyramids*. Virginia Beach, Va.: Association of Research and Enlightenment Press, 2009.

———. "Egypt's Lost Legacy and the Genesis of Civilization." *New Dawn Magazine, No. 49*, July–August, 1998.

———. *Gods of Eden*. London: Headline, 1999.

Collins, Robert M., Richard C. Doty, and Tim Cooper (contributing writer). *Exempt from Disclosure*. Vandalia, Ohio: Peregrine Communications, 2005.

"A Conversation with Matthew F. Bogdanos." *www.archaeology.org/online/interviews/bogdanos/*, October 16, 2003.

Cook, Edward M. *Solving the Mysteries of the Dead Sea Scrolls*. Grand Rapids, Mich.: Zondervan, 1994.

Cooper, Timothy S. "Suppression of Extraterrestrial Knowledge and the Translation of the Bible Conspiracy." *www.internetarchaeology.org/saufor/otherpapers/bibleconspiracy.html*, April 7, 2000.

Cooper, Timothy. "The MJ-12 Report." *www.bibliotecapleyades.net/sociopolitica/esp_sociopol_mj12_7.htm*, June 13, 1999.

Coppens, Philip. *The Ancient Alien Question*. Pompton Plains, N.J.: New Page Books, 2011.

———. "The Stargate Conundrum." *www.philipcoppens.com/starconundrum_0.html*, 2011.

"Coral Castle Demystified." *www.coralcastle.com.au/Tibetan.html*, November 27, 2010.

"Crop Circles Are Back, and This Time They're in 3-D!" *www.dailymail.co.uk/news/article-465540/Crop-circles-time-theyre-3-D.html*, July 1, 2007.

"Crop Circles." Telegram. U.S. Department of State, December 13, 2010.

D'Imperio, Mary E. *An Application of Cluster Analysis and Multidimensional Scaling to the Question of "Hands" and "Languages" in the Voynich Manuscript*, National Security Agency (undated). The document can be downloaded at the National Security Agency's Website at this link: *www.nsa.gov/applications/search/index.cfm?q=Voynich*.

———. *An Application of PTAH to the Voynich Manuscript*, National Security Agency (undated). The document can be downloaded at the National Security Agency's Website at this link: *www.nsa.gov/applications/search/index.cfm?q=Voynich*.

———. *The Voynich Manuscript: An Elegant Enigma*. Laguna Hills, Calif.: Aegean Park Press, 1978.

———. *The Voynich Manuscript: An Elegant Enigma*. National Security Agency, 1978. The document can be downloaded at the National Security Agency's Website at this link: *www.nsa.gov/applications/search/index.cfm?q=Voynich*.

Dames, Michael. *The Avebury Cycle*. London: Thames & Hudson, 1996.

David, Leonard. "EXCLUSIVE: Satellite Sleuth Closes in on Noah's Ark Mystery." *www.space.com/2134-exclusive-satellite-sleuth-closes-noah-ark-mystery.html*, March 9, 2006.

Davies, Philip R., George J. Brooke, and Philip R. Callaway. *The Complete World of the Dead Sea Scrolls*. London: Thames & Hudson, 2011.

Defense Intelligence Agency. "Analysis of 'Anomaly' on 1949 Mt. Ararat Imagery and response to FOIA taker 95-007122," July 21, 1995.

———. "Imagery of Mt. Ararat, Turkey (1949)." *www.dia.mil/public-affairs/foia/pdf/mt_ararat.pdf*, 2011.

———. *Report on the Society for Scientific Exploration conference, August 7-8, 1992*, August 14, 1992.

Defence Intelligence Staff. *Unusual Aerial Phenomena/Salisbury Plain, 1958/59*, July 30, 1978.

Defense Technical Information Center. *www.dtic.mil/descriptivesum/Y2010/DARPA/0602702E.pdf*, May 2009.

Demarest, Arthur Andrew. *Ancient Maya: The Rise and Fall of a Rainforest Civilization*. New York: Cambridge University Press, 2004.

Department of the Air Force, *AFCIN Intelligence Team Personnel*, November 3, 1961.

Department of the Navy. "Information Sheet: Philadelphia Experiment.'" *www.history.navy.mil/faqs/faq21-2.htm*, September 8, 1996.

———. "The 'Philadelphia Experiment.'" *www.history.navy.mil/faqs/faq21-1.htm*, November 28, 2000.

Devereux, Paul. "Archaeoacoustics: Spirits in the Stones." *www.forte-antimes.com/features/articles/143/archaeoacoustics_ spirits_in_the_stones.html*, October 2004.

———. "Seeing the Light." *www.forteantimes.com/features/articles/58/unidentified_atmospheric_ phenomena.html*, 2011.

———. *Stone Age Soundtracks*. London: Vega, 2001.

Dick, Steven J. "Under the Moons of Mars." *www.nasa.gov/exploration/whyweexplore/Why_We_27.html*, November 19, 2007.

Dikshitar, V.R. Ramachandra. *War in Ancient India*. New Dehli, India: Motilal Banarsidass, 1944.

Dixon, Jeane, and Rene Noorbergen. *Jeane Dixon: My Life and Prophecies*. New York: William Morrow, August 1969.

"Djinn Universe." *www.djinnuniverse.com/*, 2011.

"Dr. Andrija Puharich." *www.puharich.nl/*, 2011.

"Dr. Andrija Puharich and the Only Planet of Choice—Essential Briefings from Deep Space." *www.theonlyplanetofchoice.com/puharich.htm*, 2011.

"Dr. Wernher von Braun." *http://history.msfc.nasa.gov/vonbraun/bio.html*, 2011.

Drew, David. *The Lost Chronicles of the Maya Kings*. London: Phoenix Press, 2004.

Ebtekar, Masoumeh, and Fred Reed. *Takeover in Tehran: The Inside Story of the 1979 U.S. Embassy Capture*. Burnaby, British Columbia: Talonbooks, 2000.

"Electrogravitics: Science or Daydream?" *Product Engineering*, December 30, 1957.

Elkins, Don, Carla Rueckert, and James Allen McCarty. *The Ra Material*. West Chester, Pa.: 1984.

Elliston, Jon. "Asuang or Vampire." *www.jobernz.com/sacramentofilams/?p=850*, April 10, 2011.

"The Enterprise Mission." *www.enterprisemission.com/*, 2011.

Evanier, Mark, and Steve Sherman. *Kirby Unleashed*. Newbury Park, Calif.: Communicators Unlimited, 1972.

Farrell, Joseph P. "The Puzzle of 'The Puzzle of the Pyramids.'" *gizadeathstar.com/2011/01/the-puzzle-of-the-puzzle-of-the-space-pyramids/*, January 16, 2011.

Federal Bureau of Investigation files declassified under the terms of the Freedom of Information Act. *George W. Van Tassel, Unidentified Flying Objects*, Washington, D.C.,April 26, 1960.

Flair, Isaiah. "The Ararat Anomaly: Is This The Real Noah's Ark At Last?" *www.freerepublic.com/focus/news/667298/posts*, April 16, 2002.

Flindt, Max H., and Otto O. Binder. *Mankind: Child of the Stars*. Huntsville, Ark.: Ozark Mountain Publishing, 1999.

"Flood Legends from Around the World," *www.nwcreation.net/noahlegends.html*, 2011.

Folklore, Myths and Legends of Britain. London: The Readers Digest Association Ltd., 1973.

Genzlinger, Anna Lykins. *The Jessup Dimension*. Clarksburg, W.V.: Saucerian Press, 1981.

Geoffrey of Monmouth. "History of the Kings of Britain." *www.yorku.ca/inpar/geoffrey_thompson.pdf*, 2011.

Gerig, Bruce L. "Searching for Noah's Ark." *http://epistle.us/articles/noah.html*, 2003.

Gertz, Bill. "CIA Spy Photos Sharpen Focus on Ararat Anomaly." *Washington Times*, November 18, 1997.

Goldwater, Senator Barry. Letter to CIA Director Stansfield Turner, September 1, 1978.

———. Letter to Shlomo Arnon, March 28, 1975.

Good, Timothy. *Above Top Secret*. London: Sidgwick & Jackson, 1987.

———. *Alien Liaison*. London: Random Century Ltd., 1991.

Goodrick-Clarke, Nicholas. *Black Sun*. New York: New York University Press, 2002.

———. *The Occult Roots of Nazism*. New York: New York University Press, 1993.

"The Great Ziggurat of Dur-Kurigalzu, Aqar-Quf, Iraq." *www.skyscrapercity.com/showthread.php?t=871190*, May 15, 2009.

Grueber, H.A. *The Myths of Greece and Rome*. New York: American Book Company, 1893.

Guest, E.A. "The Other Paradigm." *Fate*, April 2005.

Guiley, Rosemary Ellen, and Philip J. Imbrogno. *The Vengeful Djinn*. Woodbury, Minn.: Llewellyn Publications, 2011.

Haddingham, Evan. "Uncovering Secrets of the Sphinx." *Smithsonian Magazine*, February 2010.

Hancock, Graham. *The Mars Mystery*. New York: Three Rivers Press, 1999.

———. *The Sign and the Seal*. New York: Touchstone Books, 1993.

Hancock, Graham, and Robert Bauval. *The Message of the Sphinx*. New York: Three Rivers Press, 1997.

Hassan, Selim. *The Sphinx: Its History in the Light of Recent Excavations*. Cairo, Egypt: Government Press, 1949.

Heron, Patrick. *The Nephilim and the Pyramid of the Apocalypse*. Dublin, Ireland: Ashfield, Press, 2004.

Higbee, Douglas. *Military Culture and Education*. Farnham, UK: Ashgate, 2010.

Hill, J. "Pyramids of Giza." *www.ancientegyptonline.co.uk/giza.html*, 2010.

Hoagland, Richard C. *The Monuments of Mars*. Berkeley, Calif.: North Atlantic Books, 2001.

Hoagland, Richard C., and Mike Bara. *Dark Mission*. Port Townsend, Wash.: Feral House Books, 2007.

The Holy Bible: English Standard Version. Wheaton, Ill.: Crossway Bibles, 2003.

Hoppe, Rand. "1958—The Face on Mars." *http://kirbymuseum.org/the-faceonmars*, March 15, 2006.

"The Huk Rebellion in the Philippines." *www.onwar.com/aced/data/papa/philippines1946.htm*, December 16, 2000.

Hungerford, Jean M. *The Exploitation of Superstitions for Purposes of Psychological Warfare*. RAND Corporation, April 14, 1950.

Hunter, Chase K. "NWO Project Blue Beam: False Holographic Second Coming." *http://2012poleshift.wetpaint.com/page/NWO+Project+Blue+Beam%3A+False+Holographic+Second+Coming*, March 9, 2010.

"J. Robert Oppenheimer, 'Now I am become death...'" *www.atomicarchive.com/Movies/Movie8.shtml*, 2011.

Jessup, Morris K. *The Case for the UFO*. New York: Citadel Press, 1955.

———. *The Expanding Case for the UFO*. New York: Citadel Press, 1957.

———. *The UFO Annual*. New York: Citadel Press, 1956.

———. *UFOs and the Bible*. New York: Citadel Press, 1956.

———. Letter to Manson J. Valentine, March 26, 1957.

"Jim Marrs Lecture on Monoatomic Gold, Part 1." *www.youtube.com/watch?v=YAGzbYxH5GQ*, May 19, 2009.

"Jim Marrs Lecture on Monoatomic Gold, Part 2." *www.youtube.com/watch?v=gSAWXSehbOc&feature=related*, May 19, 2009.

"Jim Marrs Lecture on Monoatomic Gold, Part 3." *www.youtube.com/watch?v=3XF5eDfWIN0&feature=related*, May 19, 2009.

Johnson, Obed Simon. *A Study of Chinese Alchemy.* Eastford, Conn.: Martino Publishers, 2009.

Johnson, W.J. *The Sauptikaparvan of the Mahabharata.* Oxford, UK: Oxford University Press, 1998.

Jones, Marie. *2013.* Pompton Plains, N.J.: New Page Books, 2008.

Jones, Marie, and Larry Flaxman. *The Resonance Key.* Pompton Plains, N.J.: New Page Books, 2009.

"Joseph McCabe, 1867–1955." *www.infidels.org/library/historical/joseph_mccabe/*, 2011.

Jyotirmayananda, Swami. *Mysticism of the Mahabharata.* Miami, Fla: Yoga Research Foundation, 1993.

Kasten, Len. "Is there a Disturbing Hidden Agenda in Global Events?" *Atlantis Rising, No. 41,* September/October 2003.

Kelly, Joyce. *An Archaeological Guide to Central and Southern Mexico.* Norman, Okla.: University of Oklahoma Press, 2001.

Kendrick, Sue. "Stonehenge: The Giant's Dance." *www.timetravel-britain.com/articles/stones/stonehenge1.shtml*, 2011.

Kennedy, Gerry, and Rob Churchill. *The Voynich Manuscript.* London: Orion, 2004.

Keyhoe, Donald E. *Aliens from Space.* New York: New American Library, 1974.

Kneisler, Matthew. "Noah's Ark: United States Government." *www.arksearch.com/nausgov.htm*, 2010.

Knight, Kevin. "Book of Daniel." *www.newadvent.org/cathen/04621b.htm*, 2009.

Kolata, Alan L. *The Tiwanaku.* Hoboken, N.J.: Wiley-Blackwell, 1993.

Kolb, Larry J. *Overworld.* New York: Bantam Press, 2004.

Kreisberg, Glenn (editor). *Lost Knowledge of the Ancients.* Rochester, Vt.: Bear & Company, 2010.

Kubizek, August. *The Young Hitler I Knew*. Barnsley, England: Greenhill Books, 2006.

Lamb, Andrew. "The Ararat Anomaly." *http://creation.com/the-ararat-anomaly*, March 2001.

Lambrick, George. *The Rollright Stones*. London: English Heritage, 1988.

"Lambros D. Callimahos (1910–1977)." *www.nsa.gov/about/cryptologic_heritage/hall_of_honor/2003/callimahos.shtml*, January 15, 2009.

Lansdale, Edward Geary. *In the Midst of Wars*. New York: Fordham University Press, 1991.

Lehner, Mark. *The Complete Pyramids*. New York: Thames & Hudson, 2008.

Letcher, Andy. *Shroom: A Cultural History of the Magic Mushroom*. London: Faber and Faber, 2006.

Levy, Thomas, and David Noel Freedman. "William Foxwell Albright: 1891–1971, A Biographical Memoir." *www.bibleinterp.com/articles/albright5.shtml*, February 2009.

"Ley." *www.astronautix.com/astros/ley.htm*, 2011.

Ley, Willy. *Rockets Missiles and Men in Space*. New York: Viking Press, 1968.

Liberalis, Antoninus. *The Metamorphoses of Antoninus Liberalis*. New York: Routledge, 1992.

Little, Dr. Greg, "The Brown Mountain, NC Lights Videotaped: A Field Observation—July 2003." *Alternate Perceptions Magazine*, Issue 70, July 2003.

"Looters Ransack Baghdad Museum." *http://news.bbc.co.uk/2/hi/middle_east/2942449.stm*, April 12, 2003.

Lorey, Frank."The Flood of Noah and the Flood of Gilgamesh." *www.icr.org/article/noah-flood-gilgamesh/*, 2011.

MacDonald, G. Jeffrey. "Does Maya Calendar Predict 2012 Apocalypse?" *www.usatoday.com/tech/science/2007-03-27-maya-2012_N.htm*, March 27, 2007.

MacQuarrie, Kim. *The Last Days of the Incas*. New York: Simon & Schuster, 2007.

Maestri, Nicoletta. "The Pyramid of the Magician (Mexico)." *http://archaeology.about.com/od/archaeologic7/a/Pyramid-Of-The-Magician.htm*, 2011.

Maier, Timothy W. "Anomaly or Noah's Ark?" *http://findarticles.com/p/articles/mi_m1571/is_43_16/ai_72274814/pg_2/*, November 20, 2000.

Majimdar, R.C. (editor). *The Vedic Age*. London: George Allen & Unwin, Ltd., 1951.

Mapenza, T.A. "Saddam Hussein Prophecy and Reincarnation?" *www.associatedcontent.com/article/7700786/saddam_hussein_prophecy_and_reincarnation.html*, February 8, 2011.

Marrs, Jim. "Future Technology from the Past." *www.bibliotecapleyades.net/ciencia/esp_ciencia_futuretechnology.htm*, September 2004.

"Mayan 'Apocalypse' Crop Circle Appears at Silbury Hill." *www.telegraph.co.uk/news/newstopics/howaboutthat/5777580/Mayan-apocalypse-crop-circle-appears-at-Silbury-Hill.html*. July 8, 2009.

"Mayan Myth: The Dwarf of Uxmal." *http://yucatantoday.com/en/topics/mayan-myth-dwarf-uxmal*, 2008.

McDaniel, Stanley, and Monica Rix Paxson (editors). *The Case for the Face*. Berkeley, Calif.: Adventures Unlimited Press, 1998.

McEwan, Gordon Francis. *The Incas: New Perspectives*. New York: W.W. Norton & Co., 2008.

McKillop, Heather. *The Ancient Maya*. Santa Barbara, Calif.: ABC-Clio, 2004.

Mendez, Antonio J. Mendez. "CIA Goes Hollywood: A Classic Case of Deception." *Studies in Intelligence*. Central Intelligence Agency, Winter 1999–2000.

Merkur, Dan. *The Mystery of Manna*. Rochester, Vt.: Park Street Press, 2000.

Michael, Donald N. *Proposed Studies on the Implications of Peaceful Space Activities for Human Affairs*. Washington, D.C.: Brookings Institution Press, December 1960.

Mikesh, Robert C. *Japan's World War II Balloon Bomb Attacks on North America*. Washington, D.C.: Smithsonian Institute Press, 1997.

"Milestones: 1945–1952. National Security Act of 1947." *http://history.state.gov/milestones/1945-1952/NationalSecurityAct*, 2011.

Miller, Mary, and Karl Taube. *The Gods and Symbols of Ancient Mexico and the Maya*. London: Thames and Hudson, 1993.

Monaste, Serge. "Project Blue Beam." *http://educateyourself.org/cn/projectbluebeam25jul05.shtml*, 1994.

Monteith, Dr. Henry, and Erika Monteith. *Soulmate Cosmological Action*. Bloomington, Ind.: Authorhouse, 2005.

Montgomery, Ruth. *A Gift of Prophecy*. New York: William Morrow, 1965.

Mooney, Richard E. *Colony Earth*. New York: Stein and Day, 1974.

Moore, William L. *The Roswell Investigation*. Burbank, Calif.: William L. Moore Publications and Research, 1982.

Morrison, David. "Nibiru: Armageddon Planet or Astronomical Baloney?" *http://news.discovery.com/space/david-morrison-nibiru-2012.html*, October 1, 2008.

Munro-Hay, Stuart. *The Quest For The Ark of The Covenant*. New York: I.B. Tauris & Co. Ltd., 2006.

National Security Agency. *Fields of Controversy*. January 9, 2010.

Navarra, Fernand. *Noah's Ark: I Touched It*. Plainfield, N.J.: Logos International, 1974.

Newall, R.S. *Stonehenge, Wiltshire—Ancient Monuments and Historic Buildings*. London: Her Majesty's Stationery Office, 1959.

Noorbergen, Rene. *Secrets of the Lost Races*. Ringgold, Ga.: Teach Services Inc., 2001.

Olcott, Henry S. Lecture, 1881.

Oliphant, Samuel Grant. "The Story of the Strix." *Transactions and Proceedings of the American Philological Association*. Baltimore, Md.: Johns Hopkins University Press, 1913.

"Operation Paperclip." *www.operationpaperclip.info/*, 2006.

Oppenheimer, J. Robert. *The Open Mind*. New York: Simon and Schuster, 1955.

———. *Science and the Common Understanding*. New York: Simon and Schuster, 1954.

Pais, Abraham. *J. Robert Oppenheimer: A Life*. Oxford, UK: Oxford University Press, 2006.

"Paul Devereux Speaking at the Rollright Stones: Part 1, The Dragon Project." *www.megalithic.co.uk/mm/book/devereux1trans.htm*, 2011.

"Paraphysics R&D—Warsaw Pact." Defense Intelligence Agency. Available for download at *www.earthpulse.com/epulseuploads/articles/ParaphysicsRDWarsawPact.pdf*, 1978.

"The Phobos Mysteries." *http://wiki.razing.net/ufologie.net/htm/phobswi.htm*, December 24, 2000.

"Phoenix Crop Circle May Predict End of the World." *www.telegraph. co.uk/news/newstopics/howaboutthat/5540634/Phoenix-crop-circle-may-predict-end-of-the-world.html*, June 15, 2009.

Picknett, Lynn, and Clive Prince. *The Stargate Conspiracy*. New York: Berkley Trade, 2001.

Pippin, Ed. "Tom Corbett Space Cadet." *www.solarguard.com/tchome. htm*, 2002.

Pisa, Nick. "Hitler and Stalin Were Possessed by the Devil, Says Vatican Exorcist." *www.dailymail.co.uk/news/article-402602/Hitler-Stalin-possessed-Devil-says-Vatican- exorcist.html#ixzz1f14veKKa*. August 28, 2006.

"Planet of the Apes." *www.imdb.com/title/tt0063442/*, 2011.

Pollard, Joshua, and Andrew Reynolds. *Avebury: Biography of a Landscape*. Stroud, England: The History Press, 2002.

Pringle, Heather. "Hitler's Willing Archaeologists." *www.archaeology. org/0603/abstracts/nazis.html*, Vol. 59, No. 2, March/April, 2006.

———. *The Master Plan*. New York: Hyperion, 2006.

Protzen, J.P., and S.E. Nair. "On Reconstructing Tiwanaku Architecture." *The Journal of the Society of Architectural Historians*. Vol. 59, No., 3, 2000.

Provost & Security Services. *'Unexplained Event' at Avebury, Wilts*, September 22, 1962.

Puharich, Andrija. *The Sacred Mushroom*. New York: Doubleday and Company, Inc., 1959.

———. *Uri: A Journal of the Mystery of Uri Geller*. New York: Bantam Books, 1975.

Pye, Michael, and Kirsten Dalley. *Exposed, Uncovered, and Declassified: Lost Civilizations and Secrets of the Past*. Pompton Plains, N.J.: New Page Books, 2012.

"The Pyramids of Giza Necropolis." *www.experience-ancient-egypt.com/ pyramids-of-giza.html*, 2011.

"Raiders of the Lost Ark." *www.imdb.com/title/tt0082971/*, 2011.

Randall, David. "Revealed: The Real Story Behind the Great Iraq Museum Thefts." *www.independent.co.uk/news/world/middle-east/ revealed-the-real-story-behind-the-great-iraq-museum-thefts-515067. html*, November 13, 2005.

Randles, Jenny. *UFO Crash-Landing?* London: Blandford, 1998.

Ravenscroft, Trevor. *The Spear of Destiny*. Newburyport, Mass: Weiser Books, 1982.

Recluse. "The Nine." *http://visupview.blogspot.com/2010/11/nine.html*, November 20, 2010.

Redfern, Nick. *Body Snatchers in the Desert*. New York: Paraview-Pocket, 2005.

———. *Contactees*. Pompton Plains, N.J.: New Page Books, 2009.

———. *Final Events*. San Antonio, Tex.: Anomalist Books, 2010.

———. "Is This Really Noah's Icy Tomb?" *Western Daily Press*, July 3, 2001.

———. *Keep Out!* Pompton Plains, N.J.: New Page Books, 2011.

———. *The NASA Conspiracies*. Pompton Plains, N.J.: New Page Books, 2010.

———. "Nazis, Aryans and More..." in *Mystic Utopian "Supermen"* by Edmund Shaftesbury. New Brunswick, N.J.: Global Communications, 2008.

———. "Project Moon Dust: How the Government Recovers Crashed Flying Saucers." From the *Fifth Annual UFO Crash Retrieval Conference Proceedings*. Broomfield, Colo.: Wood & Wood Enterprises, 2007.

———. *The Real Men in Black*. Pompton Plains, N.J.: New Page Books, 2011.

———. "The Sound of a UFO." *http://mysteriousuniverse.org/2011/04/the-sound-of-a-ufo/*, April 16, 2011.

———. *On the Trail of the Saucer Spies*. San Antonio, Tex: Anomalist Books, 2006.

Redfern, Nick. Interview with Mac Tonnies, March 14, 2004.

Redfern, Nick. Interview with Mac Tonnies, September 9, 2006.

Redfern, Nick, and Andy Roberts. *Strange Secrets*. New York: Paraview-Pocket Books, 2003.

Reinhard, Johan. *Machu Picchu: Exploring an Ancient Sacred Center*. Los Angeles, Calif.: Cotsen Institute of Archaeology, 2007.

Rhodes, Richard. *The Making of the Atomic Bomb*. New York: Simon & Schuster, 1986.

Richardson, Alan. *Spirits of the Stones*. London: Virgin Books, 2001.

Roberts, Andy. *Albion Dreaming*. London: Marshall Cavendish, Ltd., 2008.

Roland, Paul. *The Nazis and the Occult*. Minneapolis, Minn.: Chartwell Books, Inc., 2009.

"The Rollright Stones." *www.rollrightstones.co.uk/index.php/stones/*, 2011.

Royal Air Force. *Royal Air Force Provost & Security Services Brochure*. London: Her Majesty's Stationery Office, 1994.

Rux, Bruce. *Architects of the Underworld*. Berkeley, Calif.: Frog Ltd., 1996.

Ryan, William, and Walter Pitman. *Noah's Flood: The New Scientific Discoveries About The Event That Changed History*. New York: Simon & Schuster, 1997.

"Salisbury Plain." *www.mod.uk/DefenceInternet/AboutDefence/WhatWeDo/DefenceEstateandEnvironment/AccessRecreation/SouthWest/SalisburyPlain .htm*, 2011.

"The Salisbury Plain Training Area." *www.eng-h.gov.uk/archrev/rev95_6/salisbry.htm*, 2011

Salla, Michael. "An Exopolitical Perspective on the Preemptive War against Iraq." *www.exopolitics.org/study-paper2.htm*, February 3, 2003.

———. *Islamic Radicalism, Muslim Nations and the West*. Perth, Australia: Indian Ocean Centre for Peace Studies, 1993.

Schertel, Dr. Ernst. Magic: *History, Theory, and Practice*. Boise, Idaho: Catalog of the Universal Mind, 2009.

Schiffman, Lawrence H. *Reclaiming the Dead Sea Scrolls*. New Haven, Conn.: Yale University Press, 1995.

Schoch, Robert M. "New Studies Confirm Very Old Sphinx." *www.robertschoch.net/New%20Studies%20Confirm%20Very%20Old%20SPhinx.htm*, 2000.

———. "The Great Sphinx." *www.robertschoch.com/sphinxcontent.html*, 2011.

Schoch, Robert M., and Robert Aquinas McNally. *Pyramid Quest*. New York: Tarcher, 2005.

Schroeder, Paul. "Ancient Aliens and the Ark of the Covenant." *www.ufodigest.com/article/ancient-aliens-and-ark-covenant*, December 31, 2010.

Schul, Bill, and Ed Pettit. *Pyramid Power*. Walpole, NH: Stillpoint, 1986.

"The Scroll of Daniel." *www.biblehistory.net/newsletter/BookOfDaniel.htm, 2011.*

"Search for Noah's Ark." *www.666soon.com/search_for_noah.htm*, 2011.

Seawright, Caroline. "Wadjet, Goddess of Lower Egypt, Papyrus, and Protector of Pharaoh...." *www.thekeep.org/~kunoichi/kunoichi/themestream/wadjet.html*, November 19, 2001.

Security Service. *Examples of Ground Markings Investigated.* File reference number: WO199/1982, May 26, 1946.

Senate Select Committee on Intelligence and the Committee on Human Resources. *The Senate MK-Ultra Hearings*, Washington, D.C.: United States Printing Office, 1977.

Shafer, Byron E., and Dieter Arnold. *Temples of Ancient Egypt.* London: I.B. Tauris, 2005.

Sitchin, Zecharia. *Divine Encounters.* New York: Avon Books, 1995.

———. *The End of Days.* New York: William Morrow, 2007.

———. *Genesis Revisited.* New York: Avon Books, 1990.

———. *When Time Began.* New York: Avon Books, 1993.

Sky, Eden. "20 Questions on 2012." *www.13moon.com/prophecy%20page.htm#nav4*, 2009.

The Sleeping Prophet. "Who Was Edgar Cayce and What Are Edgar Cayce Readings?" *www.edgarcayce.org/edgar-cayce1.html*, 2011.

Soames, Nicholas, Defense Minister. Report to Martin Redmond, Member of Parliament, October 27, 1996.

Soddy, Frederick. *Interpretation of Radium.* London: J. Murray, 1912.

"The Star Gates." *www.thelivingmoon.com/42stargate/menu.html*, 2008.

"Stargate Opening over the Gulf of Aden?" *www.thegic.org/profiles/blogs/stargate-opening-over-the-gulf*, August 5, 2010.

Steiger, Brad, Alfred Bielek, and Sherry Hanson Steiger. *The Philadelphia Experiment and Other UFO Conspiracies.* New Brunswick, N.J.: Inner Light, 1990.

Steinman, William S., and Wendelle C. Stevens. *UFO Crash at Aztec.* Boulder, Colo.: UFO Photo Archives, 1986.

Stone-Miller, Rebecca. *Art of the Andes: from Chavin to Inca.* London: Thames and Hudson Ltd., 2002.

"Stonehenge, Black Giants and Magical Powers." *stonehengeguide. com/2011/02/23/stonehenge-black-giants-and-magical-powers/*, February 23, 2011.

Sutton, David. "From Deep Space to the Nine." *www.forteantimes.com/ specials/star-trek/1661/from_deep_space_to_the_nine.html*, 2011.

Svoboda, Elizabeth. "Faces, Faces Everywhere." *New York Times*, February 13, 2007.

Swift, Jonathan. *Gulliver's Travels*. Mineola, N.Y.: Dover Publications, 1996.

Temple, Robert. *The Sirius Mystery*. Rochester, Vt.: Destiny Books, 1998.

Temple, Robert, and Olivia Temple. *The Sphinx Mystery*. Rochester, Vt.: Inner Traditions, 2009.

"Tetrahedrons, Faces on Mars, Exploding Planets, Hyperdimensional Physics—and Tom Corbett, Space Cadet?! Or What Did They Know, and When Did They Know it?" *www.enterprisemission.com/corbett. htm*, 2011.

"Thebes: Amphion and Zethod Began the Wall of Thebes." *www.greek- mythology.net/modules.php?name=News&file=article&sid=19*, 2004.

Theoferrum. "Adam's Body in Noah's Ark." *http://theoferrum.hubpages. com/hub/Adams-Body-in-Noahs-Ark*, 2011.

Thompson, R. Campbell, and R. W. Hutchinson. *A Century of Exploration at Nineveh* London: Luzac and Co., 1929.

Thompson, Dr. Jeffrey. "Center for Neuroacoustic Research." *www.neu- roacoustic.com/research.html*, 2011.

Thompson, Reginald C. *Devils and Evil Spirits of Babylonia*. New York: AMS Press, Inc, 1973.

Tiltman, Brigadier, John H. *The Voynich Manuscript*. National Security Agency (undated). The document can be downloaded at the National Security Agency's Website at this link: *www.nsa.gov/applications/ search/index.cfm?q=Voynich*.

Tonnies, Mac. *After the Martian Apocalypse*. New York: Paraview-Pocket, 2004.

———. *The Cryptoterrestrials*. San Antonio, Tex.: Anomalist Books, 2010.

Trever, John C. *The Untold Story of Qumran*. Ada, Mich.: Fleming H. Revell Company, 1965.

"Unidentified Aerial Phenomena (UAP) in the UK Air Defence Region." *www.mod.uk/defenceinternet/freedomofinformation/publication-scheme/searchpublicationscheme/unidentifiedaerialphenomenauapin-theukairdefenceregion.htm*, 2011.

U.S. Air Force. *Project Blue Book Fact Sheet*, 1996.

Ussishkin, David. "Observations on Some Monuments from Carchemish." *Journal of Near Eastern Studies, Vol. 26, No. 2*, 1967.

V, Jayaram. "The Concepts of Hinduism—Amrit." *www.hinduwebsite.com/hinduism/concepts/amrit.asp*, 2010.

Van Tassel, George. *The Council of Seven Lights*. Camarillo, Calif. DeVorss and Company, 1958.

Vergano, Dan. "Maya Pyramids Pose Acoustic Riddle." *www.usatoday.com/tech/science/columnist/vergano/2010-11-14-mayan- pyramids_N.htm*, November 14, 2010.

Vermes, Geza. *The Complete Dead Sea Scrolls in English*. New York: Penguin Classics, 2004.

Verner, Miroslav. *The Pyramids: The Mystery, Culture, and Science of Egypt's Great Monuments*. New York: Grove Press. 2001.

Von Daniken, Erich. *The Eyes of the Sphinx*. New York: Berkley Trade, 1996.

———. *Odyssey of the Gods*. Pompton Plains, N.J.: New Page Books, 2012.

Von Franz, Marie-Luise. *Alchemy*. Toronto, Canada: Inner City Books, 1980.

Wagner, Stephen. "All about the Djinn." *http://paranormal.about.com/od/demonsandexorcism/a/aa060506.htm*, 2011.

Walker, Colonel Lewis H. *UFO Global Grid Theory*. Department of Defense, February 8, 1968.

Ward, Dan Sewell. "Mount Horeb." *www.halexandria.org/dward482.htm*, 2003.

Ward, Vanessa. "Nationalist Uses of the Atlantis Myth in a Nordic Framework." *http://pseudoarchaeology.org/a10-ward.html*, January 26, 2008.

Wasson, R. Gordon. *The Wondrous Mushroom*. New York: McGraw-Hill, 1980.

Webster, David L. *The Fall of the Ancient Maya*. London: Thames & Hudson, 2002.

"Who Are the Council of Nine?" *http://www.floating-world.org/council_of_nine.htm*, 2011.

Wilson, Colin. *Atlantis and the Kingdom of the Neanderthals*. Rochester, Vt.: Bear & Company, 2006.

Wingate, Richard. *Atlantis in the Amazon*. Rochester, Vt.: Bear & Company, 2011.

Wood, Bryan G., PhD. "The Walls of Jericho." *www.biblearchaeology.org/post/2008/06/the-walls-of-jericho.aspx#Article*, June 9, 2008.

Wood, Juliette. "The Holy Grail: From Romance Motif to Modern Genre." *Folklore, Vol. 111, No. 2*, October 2000.

Wood, Lamont. *Out of Place in Time and Space*. Pompton Plains, N.J.: New Page Books, 2011.

Wood, Ryan S. *Majic Eyes Only*. Broomfield, Colo: Wood Enterprises, 2005.

———. "Timothy S. Cooper." *www.majesticdocuments.com/sources/tim-cooper.php*, 2011.

Worthington, Andy. *Stonehenge: Celebration and Subversion*. Market Harborough, England: Alternative Albion, 2004.

Yenne, Bill. *Hitler's Master of the Dark Arts*. Minneapolis, Minn.: Zenith Press, 2010.

"Zab River." *http://encyclopedia2.thefreedictionary.com/Little+Zab+river*, 2011.

Zelazny, Roger. *Lord of Light*. New York: Eos, 2001.

Zubrin, Robert, and Richard Wagner. *The Case for Mars*. New York: Free Press, 1997.

INDEX

ABOUT THE AUTHOR

Nick Redfern works full-time as an author, lecturer, and journalist. He writes about a wide range of unsolved mysteries, including Bigfoot, UFOs, the Loch Ness Monster, alien encounters, and government conspiracies. He writes for *UFO Magazine, Fate,* and *Fortean Times*. His previous books include *Keep Out!, The Real Men in Black, The NASA Conspiracies, Contactees,* and *Memoirs of a Monster Hunter*. Nick has appeared on numerous television shows, including VH1's *Legend Hunters*; the BBC's *Out of this World*; History Channel's *Ancient Aliens, Monster Quest,* and *UFO Hunters*; National Geographic Channel's *The Truth About UFOs,* and *Paranatural*; and SyFy Channel's *Proof Positive*. He can be contacted at *http://nickredfernsbooks.blogspot. com.*

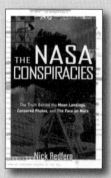
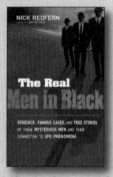